Right Away

Front cover:

Ice and Steam by Malcolm Root. The station is Marks Tey in the early 1950s and looks across to an ex Great Eastern Railway E4 class 2-4-0 locomotive from the Sudbury platform.

Right Away

The Railways of East Anglia

Douglas Bourn

This edition 2020 published by Bridge Publishing, Lowestoft, NR32 3BB, an imprint of Poppyland Ltd.

www.bridgepublishing.co.uk

ISBN 978 1 869831 33 2

Designed and typeset in 10.5 on 13.5 pt Gilamesh Pro.

Printed by Ashford Colour Press.

Picture credits:

Author's collection 1, 13, 14, 19, 21, 22, 27, 33, 40, 59, 67, 72, 73, 78, 80 (top), 98, 101, 103, 112, 118 (bottom), 119, 125, 127, 129, 131 (top), 133, 142 (bottom).
Brookbanks, B. 60*.
Butcher, D. 50.
Cambridgeshire collection 102.
Colebourne, S. 142 (top).
Crawford Holden collection 35.
F, A. 108*.
Fielding, J. 137*.
Foulger, J. & T. 139*
Great Eastern Railway Society 80 (bottom), 93, 95, 110.
Ipswich Transport Museum (Pratt, R. & Moffat. H) 90.
Newman R. 48 (bottom).
Penton, S. 57*.
Poppyland collection 48 (top), 79, 81, 96, 99, 140, 146.
Poppyland Ltd. collection 18, 20, 31, 32 (top), 54, 70, 76, 86, 87, 147.
public domain 10, 46, 71, 134, 146.
Reading, E. 36.
Ridgeway, R. 79, 81.
Robert Malster collection 44, 89, 91.
Root, M. cover, 42, 135.
Scott, P. 131 (middle top)*.
Sheppard, G. 131 (bottom)*.
Skuce, P. 131 (middle bottom)*.
Southwold Railway Trust 37, 38.
Sudbury Museum Trust 118 (top and middle).
Tansley, H.H. 99.

* under Creative Commons license.

Contents

Acknowledgements

I would like to thank the Library staff at National Railway Museum at York for their support in enabling me to access some of the wonderful archives. Members of the M & G.N. Circle, Great Eastern Railway Society, Mike Davies, volunteers on the North Norfolk Railway and East Anglian Railway Museum for providing me with evidence and access to relevant material for this volume, and finally, Hilary Alcock, John Goldsbrough, Malcolm Root, Southwold Railway Trust, Cambridgeshire Collection and Sudbury Museum Trust for their help with the illustrations. In addition I would like to thank Gareth Davies and Bridge Publishing for their support in ensuring my long treasured aim of a book about my family and the railways of East Anglia became a reality.

Douglas Bourn, 2020

Introduction

Books about railway histories are very popular. For many people, reading them and looking at photographs of old steam engines can remind them of bygone days. The continued popularity of heritage railways around the United Kingdom is another testament of this nostalgia industry.

The railways of East Anglia have been covered in many volumes.[1] There are some that focus on specific lines and periods in time. Brodribb, for example, has written three important volumes, one on the railways of the Eastern region as a whole prior to the Beeching cuts in the 1960s, one on Branch lines and one on the main lines.[2] Paye has written an excellent volume on the Southwold Railway[3], as well as, contributing to the excellent Oakwood Press series on specific branches.[4] This series also includes a well-researched volume on the Wells-Next-the Sea Branch by Jenkins[5].

Examples of recently published books on East Anglian railways.

The Midland and Great Northern Railway is however the most widely researched railway in East Anglia being the subject of numerous volumes.[6] For those more interested in the nostalgic side of the history of the railways, there have been several books on disappeared or lost lines.[7] There is also the excellent Middleton Press series that reviews individual lines, station by station.[8] However, most of them are primarily about the locomotives and the stations on the various lines. Important as these are, what is often missing are the stories of the individual railway workers and the conditions under which they worked. There are some valuable autobiographies and memories of railwaymen who worked in the region[9], but, to date, there is yet to be a volume that has aimed to bring these memories together within a broader social context.

Societies linked to heritage lines, or the promoting of past lines, also provide some valuable material.[10] Although much of this is focused primarily on technical data, some have produced important observations and stories of life on the railways. Of particular value are the resources and activities from the Midland & Great Northern (M & GN) Circle and the Great Eastern Railway Society. Both produce informative newsletters and occasional publications.

This volume aims to address the gap by bringing to life stories of railway workers within a context of the changing nature of the industry from the mid-19th century to the present day. It brings together some of the literature of these memoirs, plus verbal testimonies, some of which were recorded as part of the research for this volume, alongside evidence from railway magazines and local and regional newspapers. This volume has also been heavily influenced by my personal and family memories and most of the chapters have a link to my own experiences.

Strangleman has reviewed the literature on railway history and noted the criticisms of much of this work for wallowing in nostalgia and romanticism.[11] Robbins has noted that historians have tended to ignore the broader social and economic influence of railways.[12] There is some justifiable criticism of the more autobiographical studies for promoting a past 'golden age' and ignoring the harsh conditions and low wages railwaymen had to work under. But, at the same time, there needs to be some assessment of why this nostalgia is popular and why railwaymen themselves often talk and write about positive past experiences. This, I would suggest, is in part due to a sense of loss of identity which has been acerbated by privatisation and the loss of a sense of collective ways of working. For example, the train driver today has a very isolated existence. Based in their cab with no companion, often having to do three different tasks—driver, guard and announcer.

Ernest Bourn, the author's father, in his driver's uniform by his diesel multiple unit at Sudbury Station in the early 1970s.

Strangleman suggests that memories, autobiographies and stories of working lives of railwaymen can provide an authentic voice. I aim in this volume to look critically at a range of memoirs and autobiographies and situate them within a broader discussion of the literature and evidence from primary sources, such as railway journals and official reports and my family's own direct experience.

I grew up in a railway family. My father was a train driver based at Sudbury in Suffolk for most of his working life. He met my mother in Melton Constable, a village built on the railway, during the Second World War. Her father, my grandfather, worked at Melton station as a wheeltapper. Much of my childhood and early adulthood was therefore heavily influenced by the railways.

But this volume does not seek to wallow in nostalgia. While references will be made to my own personal experiences and the rationales for specific chapters and themes, what I aim to cover is the lives of people working on the railways and the impact they had on local communities, economies and cultures. As will become evident upon reading this volume, I am not calling for a return to a bygone age. The railway industry today, despite the ravages of the Beeching cuts era in the 1960s and privatisation, has never been as healthy and popular as it is today. The importance of travelling by rail has been heightened by the awareness of the ways we are polluting the planet through petroleum and diesel fuelled cars and aeroplanes. We should not forget that the steam era, through its use of coal and smoke, was a contributor to pollution. I can remember that even in the 1950s some of the major stations such as London Liverpool Street were permanently shrouded in smoke. My father, who had started work on the railways as a cleaner and then progressed to fireman and eventually driver, continually suffered from the effects of inhaling smoke and soot until the arrival of diesel in the late 1950s.

What inspired me to write this volume was to record the ways in which railway workers coped with appalling working conditions, low wages and an autocratic and almost feudal management style. The first trade union for railway workers, later to become the National Union of Railwaymen, was first called the Amalgamated Society of Railway Servants (ASRS). This gives an indication of their status in the 19th century. What is also noticeable from reading and listening to oral histories of railway workers is that, despite these conditions, there was a great sense of pride in their work. Readers will find out about great heroic stories of railway workers, saving the lives of the general public while working all hours.

Histories of railways, particularly if they are focused on a specific region of the country, can provide important contributions to our broader social, economic and cultural understanding that goes beyond nostalgic insights into how people lived. The railways transformed the lives of people and economies in the UK. Goods transported quickly to market enabled a much broader range of fresh food being available in the bigger cities. Economies grew with the easy transportation of goods. This was particularly the case in the 19th and early 20th centuries for an industrialised country like the UK. Iron, steel and coal, the bedrock of many industries, became available across the country. The railways also opened up opportunities for greater social mobility. Working class people, for the first time, could afford to travel and visit friends and relatives and enjoy the countryside and seaside. This mobility also reflected a broader and perhaps even more important transformation, the gradual democratisation of the movement of peoples. Whilst there remained different classes of trains, the divisions between social classes through using the same trains had a major impact upon social life. Working class people could feel included in societies and economies.

East Anglia is chosen as the focus for this volume for personal, social and economic reasons. It is the region within which I grew up and is an area with which I am familiar. I know most of the lines and stations well.

East Anglia is also a region that brings together the impact of industrial development, agriculture, fishing and tourism. Whilst the region needed to import iron and coal from other parts of the country, as a result of the growth of the railways it became a major focus for a number of specialist industries. It is a region that has grown in size from being a predominantly rural area with two or three main centres of population to having several important economic centres, as well as important commuter routes.

For the purposes of this volume, my focus is primarily on Norfolk and Suffolk with occasional reference to, and inclusion of, examples from Cambridgeshire and North Essex. This is, in part, personal as they include the direct experience of the counties where my father and grandfather worked. They are also the counties which demonstrate several of the major themes of this volume: the impact of the railways on the nature of the rural economy and the growth of holiday resorts.

This volume represents a conscious decision to be a distinct break from many published books to date on railways in East Anglia by not only celebrating the stories of railway workers but also bringing in personal connections and situating them within a generalised social and economic context. It is not about how railways worked or even about specific locomotives, apart from one chapter, but about the people who worked on them and represents a contribution to a broader social and economic history of the region. Whilst I hope railway enthusiasts will read and enjoy this volume, it is aimed at a much wider readership.

The structure of the volume is broadly chronological and focuses on particular themes and places. The rationale for some of these is personal like the chapters on Melton Constable, Stour Valley line and Manningtree. But they are also chosen because they illustrate broader themes, such as the impact on communities, changes in government policies or the social and economic purpose of specific stations.

Following this introduction, chapters one, two and three provide a summary of the growth of the railways in East Anglia focusing on their social and economic impact. A theme of these chapters is the way in which the railways, like many industries in the 19th century, were subject to fluctuating economic forces and the drive for profit and wealth by the company's owners and managers. The lives of the workers on the other hand were very hard. Whilst it is outside of the scope of this volume, the conditions under which the railway navvies constructed the lines were appalling and this has been well documented elsewhere.[13]

Chapters four and five outline the rise and impact of tourism and the holiday season on the railways in East Anglia. The region benefits from some of the best beaches in the UK and a relatively warm and dry climate. It is also a region with a number of important ports. Railways played an important part in their development. A specific chapter is given to Lowestoft. It not only exemplifies these developments well, but is also a town where I have close personal associations. My father was born there and his parents and brothers and sisters all grew up in the town, and many of their descendants still live there today.

Chapters six and seven summarise the history and working lives of people who worked on the main artery line in the region from London to Norwich, and the role and changing nature of the three stations that once existed in Norwich, the regional capital and largest city.

Melton Constable is the subject of chapter eight. This small village in North Norfolk became, by the end of the 19th century, the railway capital of the region, with four different lines going through what became an important junction and hub for passengers and freight. It is also chosen as a chapter because of the family connections mentioned earlier and where I spent a lot of my childhood holidays.

A specific chapter is given to Harwich on the North East Essex coast. Harwich became one of the principal gateways to Europe via ferries to the Hook of Holland and therefore acted as an important port to open up East Anglia to the cultures and economies of mainland Europe.

Chapter ten reviews the impact of the Second World War. The war had a major impact on the railways of East Anglia. The region was host to a large number of airfields and was in the frontline for conflict with Nazi Germany.

Chapter eleven is perhaps the one nostalgic chapter focusing on a specific steam locomotive, the Britannia class; the flagship engine for the main London to Norwich line in the 1950s and later for trains to the coastal resorts and ports. It was for me, as a child, the locomotive you always looked out for when you were travelling by train, and like many a trainspotter at the time, your aim was to get the names and the numbers of all of them.

The 1950s and 1960s were very difficult times for the railway industry, with chronic under investment, poor management and a return to the days of the profit being the primary motive. Although it was the era of the positive transition from steam to diesel and electric, it is best remembered for the Beeching era when savage cuts were made, with the closure of the majority of small rural lines. East Anglia was one of the worst hit regions because it had so many of these small rural lines. Although acting as a lifeblood for many communities, they were deemed unpopular. These themes form the focus of chapter twelve. Chapter thirteen goes one step further and looks in detail at one line, the Stour Valley line between Cambridge and Marks Tey, near Colchester. Of all the lines I discuss, this line is perhaps the most personal to me. A key point on the line was Sudbury which is where I was born and brought up. It is where my father was based as first a fireman and later a driver from the mid 1940s to his retirement in the 1970s. He played a central role in the campaign for retaining the line and was partially successful, as the line from Sudbury to Marks Tey remained opened. It is in part due to his hard work and background research for the leading campaigners that the line has remained open and is, today, a very profitable one. For me, this line was my route and link to the wider UK and beyond.

The next section looks at the changing nature of railways within the region from the 1980s to the present day and focuses on three main themes. Chapter fourteen looks at the ways in which the railways have changed since the move to privatisation and the impact this has had on working patterns and workers' relationship to the industry. The following chapter looks at an example, Manningtree, that demonstrates the importance of the railways to the regional economy. I have a personal connection to this station, as it has been my home station for several years and is today the hub for many hundreds of commuters to London everyday.

The final chapter, before a short conclusion, is on the heritage lines of East Anglia which remind people about the history of the railways in the region and also act as important contributors to local economies. Some, such as the East Anglian Railway Museum on the Stour valley line at Chappel, operate mainly to provide information about the local line. Others, such as the North Norfolk line from Sheringham to Holt, provide an important tourist attraction for families on holiday at the coast.

I conclude the volume with some personal reflections on the importance of the railways to myself, my family and to local communities. As will become evident whilst reading this volume, I am great supporter of railways and love travelling by train. However I also show that the railways of East Anglia have had their difficulties. Today the railway lines that still exist are well used. On some days, on some of the services, even to get a seat is a challenge. This situation exists because of historic under investment that has continued into the 21st century and is only now being rectified with the introduction of new trains in

2020.

Notes

1 *These include Allen (1955), Gordon (1990 ed.), Gale (2015), Joby (1987). Moffat's (1987) study of the first railways and the influence of Peter Bruff and Barney's Norfolk Railway book (2007) on Railway Mania in East Anglia from 1834 to 1862 are amongst the more academically researched volumes.*

2 *Brodribb (1994), (2000), (2009).*

3 *Paye (2018).*

4 *Paye: Aldeburgh Branch (2012), Snape Branch (2005), Hadleigh Branch (2006), Framlingham Branch (2008) and Mellis and Eye Railway (2012).*

5 *Jenkins (2011).*

6 *Digby (2014, 2015), Essery (2009) Clark (1967), Wrottesley(1981).*

7 *Oppitz (1989), Wallis (2011).*

8 *Some of the most relevant to this volume are Adderson and Kenworthy (1998, 2007, 2011), Mitchell and Smith (1984), Mitchell (2011, 2012).*

9 *Baker (2019), Freestone and Smith (1998), Harvey (1986) Hewison (1981), Morris (2012), Robinson (2005), Marriott (1974) and Taylor (2008).*

10 *http://www.mgncircle.org.uk; https://www.gersociety.org.uk; http://www.norfolkrailwaysociety.org.uk; http://ipswichanddistricthistoricaltransportsociety.co.uk/index.html; https://www.facebook.com/Norwich-City-Station-Preservation-GroupFONCS-171276892893836/?ref=page_internal*

11 *Strangleman (2002).*

12 *Robbins (1967).*

13 *Coleman (2000), Burton (2016), https://www.christianwolmar.co.uk/2011/12/the-railway-navvies/*

Shoreditch station, December 1850.

Landscape, Economies and the Coming Of The Railway

East Anglia at the beginning of the 19th century was a rural region, relying predominantly on agricultural produce for its wealth. What it did have however, was a number of ports, not only those by the sea, like Kings Lynn, Yarmouth, Lowestoft, Aldeburgh, Harwich and Maldon, but inland ports, which were navigable by large barges. These included Ely, Norwich, Ipswich and even Cambridge. Only Bury St. Edmunds of the large towns had no direct access to water-borne freight traffic.

Its economy was based on grain and, in the coastal areas, fishing. There was no major manufacturing base. The region had no coal or iron, and the majority of the population lived in the countryside. In the 1840s, industrial activity was usually small scale and local. Most industries, such as milling, malting, brewing and the manufacturing of agricultural implements, were dependent on access to the soil. In the early decades of the 19th century the economy of the region was weak. Agriculture had suffered from the post-1815 slump in corn prices and there was a reduction in demand for local wool. Norwich, the main city in the region, was also in economic decline during this period.

Journeys with goods from Norwich to London would take two days by stagecoach and this meant that the region had little direct engagement with the rest of the country. There were also paddle steamers from main ports down to London, but these were not always reliable.

East Anglia was therefore predominantly an agriculturally based economy in the early 19th century and much of the land in the region was owned by wealthy landowners who provided only minimal investment into the local communities. The status and employment opportunities for rural workers had declined during the late 18th and early 19th centuries. Enclosures, increased mechanisation and rising prices left many rural workers destitute. This led to considerable social unrest, as can be seen from numerous riots in the region during this period. The most famous of these were the 'Captain Swing' riots of 1830/31 that took place across England in opposition to the growing mechanisation of farming, in particular, the introduction of threshing machines, each one replacing ten labourers. East Anglia was one of the leading areas in the country for these riots and its legacy could be seen in the beginnings of rural trade unionism and support for Chartism, in Norwich in particular, during in the 1830s.

Agricultural labourers were therefore always looking for additional forms of employment. Many of them turned to constructing canals and became known as 'navvies', derived from the word 'navigation'. This also meant that, when the railways began to be constructed in the region, there was a ready-made and willing workforce.

The First Railways

The first railways that were developed in England were in the rising industrial regions of the North with easy access to coal. However, at the same time as the first passenger railway was being constructed from Stockton to Darlington (opened 1825), discussions were taking place in other regions to establish rail connections. In East Anglia plans were drawn up for lines from London to Cambridge and London to Ipswich, but they came to nothing.[1]

It was not until the early 1830s that proposals were put to Parliament for a line from London to Norwich. All railway proposals at this time had to go through a very lengthy process in order to gain approval. An Act of Parliament needed to be passed and, as virtually all Members of Parliament (MPs) at this time from an area like East Anglia were landowners, this was not going to be an easy task. Whilst there was increasing acceptance of the value of railways for industrial areas, having a railway in a rural area raised major questions. Landowners were not the only sceptics, the local and regional press also influenced public opinion. One newspaper argued that, since much of the region's economy was based on the sea, the railway would destroy what had been seen as one of the main bulwarks of East Anglian life.

Arguments in favour of railways centred on the concepts of speedy transportation of fish to inland markets, the cost of transporting animals, the use of the ports to bring coal inland and quick access to London.

Various attempts were made in the 1830s for a railway to connect East Anglia with London and the rest of the country. Key to these developments was the drive for a line from London to York with suggestions of a route via Cambridge and a branch to Norwich. It was however the financial support of wealthy regional businessmen, notably J.C. Cobbold, that led to the formation of the first company to build a line across the region. Despite some

John Chevallier Cobbold.

landowner opposition, the Bill to enable construction to start passed through the House of Commons and then the Lords in the summer of 1836. The argument that it would aid the development of trade to, and agriculture in, the region won the day.

After several false starts, the construction of the Eastern Counties Railway (ECR), as it became called, with a plan to link London to Norwich, began in the spring of 1837. Costs soon exceeded estimates, and, by the following year, work had only progressed between Mile End, in East London, and Brentwood. The first ten miles of this line from Mile End to Romford opened for passenger traffic on 20th June 1839 with another seven miles into Shoreditch in London and out to Brentwood opening in July 1840. Shoreditch remained the terminus for the line until 1874/5 when Liverpool Street was opened. But the inexperience of those running this line showed its fragility. Within a few weeks of opening, there were several major accidents including one at Brentwood, when the engine ran out of control, costing the lives of the driver and fireman. This accident was typical of many at the time, with the drivers having very little experience.

In addition to the lack of experience amongst the railway workforce at this time, there were two other factors that had a major bearing on the growth of the system. Constructing a railway at this time required support from local landowners and investors, and the directors of this Eastern Counties Railway encountered problems with both parties. The construction of the line to Chelmsford began, but its extension to Colchester took until 1843 given the need to raise more capital, poor weather and the necessity to built several bridges. By 1845 the line had reached Ardleigh on the borders of Essex and Suffolk.

The second factor was the attitude of the newspapers. Most of the newspapers in the region in the 1830s had opposed the introduction of railways. The basis of their opposition ranged from notions of protecting rural communities to defending the value of ports and seafaring.[2] However, by the middle of 1840, opinion was changing towards the railways. People and businesses could see the benefits and as this changed the view of many local newspapers. In Norfolk, for example, the *Norwich Mercury* began supporting the introduction of railways to and from the city.[3] The railways represented both commercial expansion and new opportunities for investment. They had begun to capture the public imagination.

By the early 1840s, there was growing interest in the development of several lines across East Anglia, including joining Cambridge to Norwich, extending the line from Colchester to Norwich and lines to connect Bury St Edmunds and Yarmouth to Norwich.

Meanwhile another company, the Northern and Eastern, had secured approval for a line from London to Cambridge and then hopefully to Norwich. This line took four years to get as far as Bishop's Stortford, and by 1842, was still some way short of Cambridge.

In 1843 and 1844 the two companies merged under the leadership of the Eastern Counties. Whilst the extension from Colchester northwards to Ipswich stalled, progress was made on the other line and construction began in 1844 for an extension from Bishop's Stortford through Cambridge to Ely and Brandon.

It is important to note that the construction of a railway line had a major impact upon the local economy. Many lines built in the 1840s often employed large numbers of workers, albeit for short periods of time. Whilst local men ended up being employed on the railways, the evidence from Gordon's research suggests that the majority of the workmen came from outside of the region and were likely to be former canal navvies, as well as former coachmen and migrants from Ireland.[4] Most were itinerant workers who moved around from construction job to construction job. For example, as Gordon has shown in his research on the development of railway lines around Kings Lynn:

> ...between September 1846 and the opening of the L & E some thirteen months later there would be about 5,000 workers of all kinds employed on the railway and within easy reach of King's Lynn.[5]

A common complaint in the local press was the behaviour of these navvies. For example, in 1862, the *Ipswich Journal* reported the disorderly and drunken conduct associated with the men:

> Last Sunday week I am told that drunken navvies were parading the street in parties of four or five together, the conduct and language was most disgraceful, they accosted any female they happened to meet.[6]

However, it should be noted that some of the leading contractors of railway development in the Eastern region, such as Samuel Peto and Thomas Brassey, supported their workers by establishing funds for sick workers and their families and did not condone such rowdiness.

The various companies were indeed run on very autocratic lines with a strong emphasis on formal uniforms and the promotion of law and order. The engineer of the company would be responsible for the effective maintenance and running of the track, the engines and carriages and the driver and firemen. The running of the stations was in the hands of what were then called the railway police with each station having their own sergeant. On the trains were conductors and guards. Both the railway police and the guards at first wore top hats and bright uniforms which mimicked a military outlook.

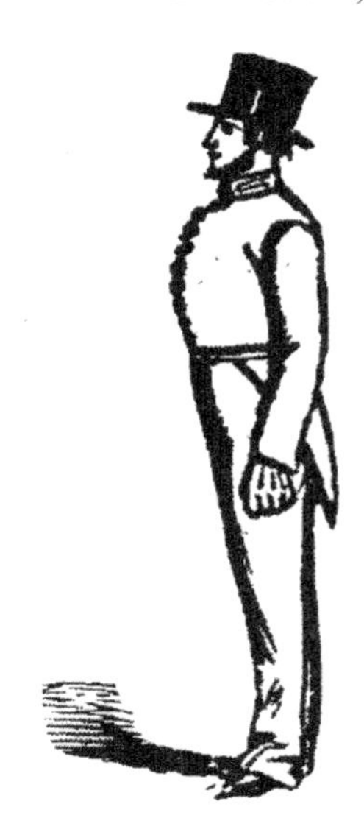
Early railway policeman.

The railway police, in these early years, had a particularly difficult job with unruly behaviour at stations. In some places, it became necessary to engage extra police to protect stations and passengers. At Ipswich station, for example, there was a complement of fourteen policemen, the majority of whom were also porters.

In these early years, the railways provided a form of permanent and secure employment, something that a largely agriculturally based economy had not been able to offer. Skilled labour was difficult to find among the general workforce. These early, uneducated, drivers and firemen of these steam locomotives had to learn their trade on the job. The work was very challenging. The locomotives were open to all weathers and had only very rudimentary braking systems. Every train also had a guard, who was responsible for the safety of the train by ensuring the main brakes worked, all lamps were attached and lit and all the carriages were clean. It has been suggested that guards on the railways in East Anglia in the mid- and late- 19th century were highly regarded, 'he looks after you as carefully as the parcels in the van'.[7]

An example of the challenges guards had in these early years can be seen in these memories from Neele:

> The brakes of the trains were worked from the roof of the carriages, the guards riding outside, in an unprotected seat at the end of the vehicle, applying the brake by turning on the hand screw. A journey from Wymondham to Dereham cured my desire to travel outside railway carriages. At the end of the train were two of the vehicles with outside seats for the guard. ...The guard, an old stager, sat on the one which enabled him to turn his back to the engine, while I, as a novice, sat opposite, facing him. The dust, the smoke, steam, and smother, which filled my eyes, ears, and nose during that short ride, were sufficient to put a stop to any wish for further experience in that direction...[8]

The early railway coaches reflected the class divisions that dominated much of Victorian England with comfortable first-class coaches and basic second and third classes.

During this time, The Eastern Counties Railway was also known as dangerous and unreliable. For example, the magazine *Punch* suggested that every criminal waiting to be executed should have their sentence exchanged for a journey on the line. It was called the 'pariah of the railways'.[9] An example of the ways in which the ECR was seen is revealed from the following extract from *Punch*:

> A self-confident passenger, enraged at what he considered the gross incompetence or negligence of the company, was in the habit, whenever he went on a journey, of distributing clever cartoons holding up the company to derision. One of these represented a costermonger with his donkey and barrow, racing and outrunning the train. Another, still bolder in its conception, showed the coster in his barrow driving along the line with his donkey, apparently going about eleven miles an hour. The donkey is pulling the train, the engine, which is fastened to the coster's cart by a long chain. The engine-driver is sitting asleep on the tender; flying from the engine is a flag bearing the letters "E.C.R." and a kicking donkey; and on the guidepost astride the arm pointing to London, sits Mr. Punch with his finger on his nose.[10]

Some of the most illuminating extracts concerning the working life of an employee can be found in Neele's, *Notes Of A Railway Superintendent.* For example, the experience of his first day at Ely, in the late 1840s, shows an astonishing lack of supervision:

> ...In the booking office at Ely Station, my first attempt at issuing tickets without supervision was made in the absence of the upper clerk who was training me. He was late coming on duty, and in order to advance matters I booked the passengers who were waiting for the train. Unfortunately, I issued "penny per mile" tickets instead of the "3rd class," which in those days were, on some lines, obtainable by trains not appointed to call at every station. My instructor came in at the last moment, and, discovering the mistake, at once rushed to the platform and obtained, fortunately for me and for himself, the difference in cash from the passengers, and exchanged the erroneous tickets for correct ones.[11]

Neele later worked as a Clerk at Bishopsgate station in London and it was here he noted the strong 'militaristic' management culture. Most managers he said came from a naval or military background:

> There was always a tendency to the martinet in the military man, and to quarter-deck discipline with the naval autocrats.[12]

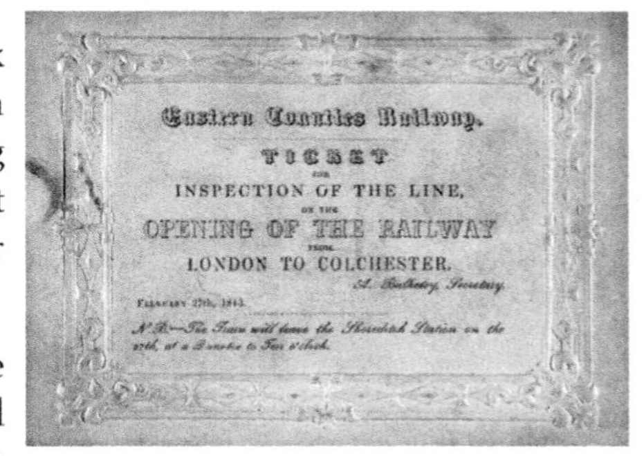

ECR special ticket for the launch of railway, 1843.

An example of the everyday hazards and lack of safety regulations could be seen in this note from Neele:

> I had occasion to convey some communication from head-quarters (Bishopsgate) to the offices at Brick Lane. The shortest way was along the line, and the office messenger undertook to pilot me over the dangerous track. We arrived safely, and he left me to make my return unaccompanied. My mission completed, I had to make my way back, and on leaving the goods shed it was necessary to pass on to the main line. I had no idea of the nearness of the rails. Going through the doorway, I was in the act of stepping on to the line, when a passenger engine and train rushed by. The running line closely adjoined the Goods Shed wall, and by these few seconds my railway career was most providentially not abruptly terminated on the spot. There should certainly have been some caution or warning exhibited. It was my last walk along that portion of the line.[13]

Neele's memoirs also show that, despite the appalling conditions many of the men had to work under and the rather autocratic styles of management, there was respect and mutual support amongst the workforce. When men were injured or killed on the lines, an all too frequent occurrence, men would always rally round and provide funds for the widows and families and made sure there was a good turnout at funerals.

Although many men valued working on the railways, the autocratic style of management tended to lead to conflicts and disputes. In the early years of the railways there were no trade unions but the workforce, because of their sense of collective solidarity, were often prepared to air their grievances. One example was a strike on the Eastern Counties in 1839 when the drivers, firemen and platelayers complained about their poor wages. Fortunately, an agreement was easily reached but, as will be shown later, this was not always the case. In the late 1840s with railway companies suffering financial difficulties, attempts were made to reduce workers' salaries. Lower paid men had their wages cut by ten per cent but, at least some of the senior managers, also had to take salaries reductions.[14]

All railways, including those in East Anglia, were run on rather amateurish lines. There were no rule books or guidelines to follow and men had to develop their own skills on the job. Lines emerged in a very haphazard manner, often competing with each other, and with no overall plan or vision. East Anglia was however fortunate. From the 1840s onwards there were some influential engineers and businessmen who had a clear perception for the future.

Notes

1 *Moffat (1987).*

2 *see Barney (2007), Gale (2015).*

3 *Moffat (1987) p.10.*

4 *Gordon (1964).*

5 *Gordon (1964) p.285.*

6 *Quoted in Gale (2015) p.2.*

7 *Ibid. p.21.*

8 *Neele (1904) p.11.*

9 *Quoted in Pendeleton (1896) p.377.*

10 *Ibid. pp.377-378.*

11 *Neele p.2.*

12 *Ibid. p.8.*

13 *Ibid. p.9.*

14 *Moffat (1987).*

From Eastern Counties and Eastern Union to Great Eastern

The Influence of the Stephensons

East Anglia, like all England, was helped by the overwhelming interest in railway development in the mid-1840s. This 'railway mania', as it became called, is commonly associated with George Hudson but, before we get to discuss his influence, one should note that two of the most famous engineers in the early development of railways, George and Robert Stephenson, also played an important role in the region.

George and his son Robert were, by the 1840s, regarded as the most influential railway figures in the country. Not only had George overseen the building of the famous 'Rocket' engine for the Liverpool and Manchester railway in 1830, but together with Robert, he had built railways throughout England. In 1842 George and Robert saw major opportunities in East Anglia and they put their names behind plans for a line between Norwich and Yarmouth. They saw this line as the first stage in constructing a direct route from London to Norwich. The addition of their names to the proposal meant it was easy to attract investors. George became Chairman of the Board and Robert chief engineer.[1]

Despite George Stephenson complaining constantly about the lack of funds to support the development of the line, and the opposition of local landowners, it was due mostly to his efforts that the line opened in 1844 with seven trains each way for a fifty-minute journey.[2]

At the same time, the Norfolk Railway had been constructing a line from Norwich to Brandon which opened in 1845. Support for this line was helped by the endorsement of Norwich's city mayor and the *Norfolk Mercury*. The engineers of the Norwich & Brandon line were George's son, Robert Stephenson, and George Parker Bidder, who later became Chairman of the Norfolk Railway Company.

Rise and Fall of George Hudson

George Hudson was already well known within the railway industry by the time he became Chairman of Eastern Counties Railway (ECR) in the mid-1840s. He already had a reputation as a leading entrepreneur in the promotion of

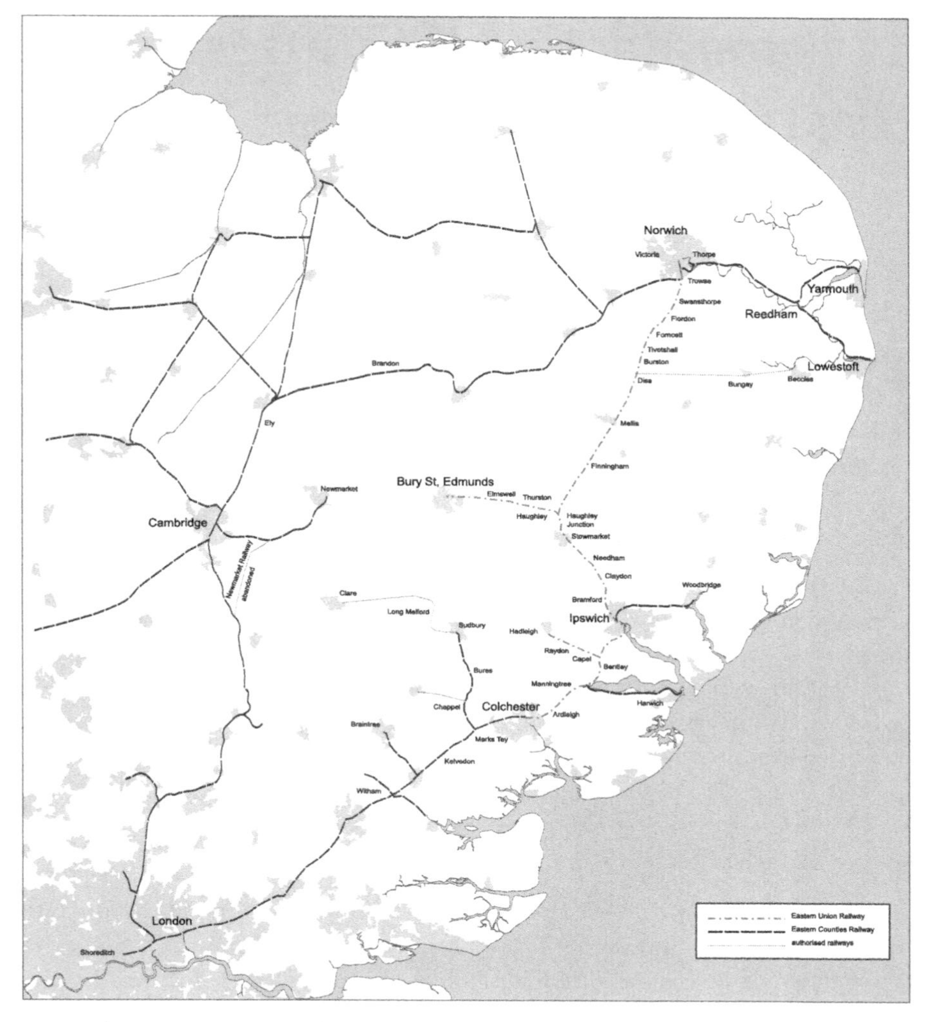

Map 1. The Eastern Counties and Union Railways, themselves the result of previous amalgamations.

railway lines around the country. He had become known as the 'railway king' and saw the ECR as an important stepping stone in ensuring a direct route from London to Doncaster and York via Cambridge. He already held the chairmanship of many companies and for a couple of years there was expansion of many lines. This 'railway mania' resulted in a number of projects being proposed with Acts to Parliament being submitted in 1846. These included:

- Norwich to Dereham
- Norwich to Cromer, later restricted to Aylsham and North Walsham

- Ipswich to Beccles with then one to Norwich via Bungay and the other to Lowestoft
- Thetford to Bury and Newmarket
- Newmarket to Chesterford
- Spalding to Brandon.

George Hudson.

Other companies proposed extension of the line from Bury to Haughley and Norwich, Maldon to Thetford, Maldon to Bury, Walthamstow to Thetford via Dunmow and Bury, Yarmouth to Diss, Norwich to Dereham with branches to Fakenham.

Many of these proposals aimed to link towns to either a main line to London, or, across country to Peterborough and therefore the Midlands and the North.

Although many of these lines did eventually materialise, Hudson had clearly been over ambitious in his plans. Not only did he overextend his credit, his expansion plans came at a time when the country was entering an economic depression. As a consequence, the fortunes of the ECR were in serious decline. Hudson's empire collapsed as a result of greediness and corruption and the company looked to its competitors to survive. But as Beaumont shows in his biography of Hudson, there was a lot of double dealing and hypocrisy going on within the boards of the railway companies at the time and that, to a certain extent, the 'railway king' was just typical of many at the time.[3]

Peter Bruff: the Brunel of the Eastern Counties

A major figure in resolving the disputes and imposing priorities on the situation, was Peter Bruff. Bruff's background was as a shipping engineer but he learnt about railway construction from Joseph Locke, who had worked with George Stephenson on the Liverpool to Manchester railway.

Although first employed by the Eastern Counties Railway, he appears to have fallen out with them in 1842 deciding to launch a rival company, the Eastern Union Railway (EUR). He had the support of Cobbold who had been involved in the early development of the Eastern Counties. Cobbold was based in Ipswich and used his power base there to secure funds to establish the EUR.

Bruff was a very ambitious engineer and was not afraid to propose what, at the time, were considered outlandish schemes.[4] The most ambitious of these being the construction of a tunnel at Ipswich to gain a quick and straight passage northward. After considerable debate, both in the region and within Parliament, his proposal was accepted, and construction of the line north of Ipswich towards Norwich began.

Norwich to London via Brandon

As suggested in the previous chapter, building routes from London outwards was slow. There was progress in the west of the region with a line from Bishops Stortford to Brandon, meeting the Norfolk Railway from Norwich, and joining up to Ely and Peterborough. This resulted in links to the Midlands and the North enabling coal from the North to be transported into the region.

Brandon station, 1845.

1844 was a key year in the development of the region's railway network. The line from Yarmouth to Norwich opened on April 30 1844 providing a regular service of four trains per day in each direction. Work began in that year on Norwich to Brandon which would eventually link to Cambridge and Bishops Stortford and then on to London. By the end of 1845 there was a direct link from Norwich to London, although not by the envisaged route through Ipswich and Colchester, but via Ely and Cambridge.

With viable lines west from Norwich and east to Yarmouth, the companies running these lines merged in 1845 to form the Norfolk Railway Company.[5]

From Colchester to Norwich

The planned London to Norwich line via Colchester and Ipswich, struggling for funds, had only reached Colchester by 1843. This is where Cobbold and Peter Bruff become important in providing both the funds and the expertise. Building the line from Ipswich to Colchester was a major challenge, with the need for a major bridge over the River Stour and the creation of several deep cuttings.

Work began on the line in August 1844 and its construction is a good example of many of the issues workmen faced in building a railway. The vast majority of those employed on constructing the line came from the local area reflecting the parlous state of the agricultural economy. Working and living conditions were rudimentary and, by the summer of 1845, there were about a thousand workers in shanty towns on the side of the line. There were numerous incidences of unruly behaviour and accidents with, sadly, some fatalities. Ten lives were lost, including three working on the construction of the tunnel at Ipswich. Several of the worst injuries came as a result of horse-drawn wagons tipping over and crushing workers. The extent of the accidents and injuries even led to coroners' reports asking why there were no travelling hospitals provided for the workforce.[6]

Brantham cutting construction, on the line between Manningtree and Ipswich.

Special excursions to introduce people to train travel were a feature of the marketing and promotion when the line became operational. These publicity campaigns often underestimated the naivety of the travellers. This happened early in 1845 soon after the opening of the line to Ipswich. A train hauled by two engines had over a thousand passengers on board:

Colchester station soon after its opening.

> All went well until Brentwood was reached where some speed having been worked up the enginemen saw a goods wagon in their path. After whistling, applying the brakes and reversing the engines, they jumped off followed by the Foreman. Fortunately owing to the speed being low one was hurt and the journey continued after a two-hour delay.[7]

Extension to Bury and on to Norwich

A Bill for an extension to Bury St. Edmunds received royal assent in July 1845 and this is again where the skills of Bruff became important.

To construct this line meant building a tunnel out of Ipswich which was 361 yards in length and had to be built on a curve. Despite numerous difficulties with water seepage and tensions in the workforce, the tunnel was completed by November 1846. Later that month the first train went from Ipswich to Bury via Stowmarket.

The completion of this line allowed for the construction of the spur from

Stowmarket north to Norwich. Work began on the line in February 1847 and, by the summer of that year, over twelve hundred men were involved in the construction of the line. The building of this line, at a time of economic recession, and subsequent collapse of investment in new railways, eventually saw the Eastern Union and the Norfolk Railway agree to amalgamate.

Another major issue was the terminus in Norwich and the difficulties in building a railway line over the marshy terrain just south of the city centre. Eventually, this was resolved with the creation of a terminus at Victoria Gardens. The opening of the line took place in December 1849 but in order to link to the line to the west of Norwich a link via Trowse was built and completed in 1851. Further details about this terminus are discussed in chapter seven.

Expansion of the Network

As already mentioned, a line had been created to Bury St. Edmunds and around the same time construction began on other lines, including from Colchester to Sudbury with a branch at Chappel to Halstead. Another line built during this period was one via Newmarket linking Cambridge with Bury and Ipswich. By end of 1846, lines were planned between Norwich - Aylsham - North Walsham, Thetford - Reedham - Bury, Ipswich - Woodbridge - Norwich to Dereham.

There were numerous accidents in these early rail developments. As Moffat notes:

> The first accident to a passenger train occurred only the day after the Norwich line opened. It was getting dark by the time the 2.15pm from Victoria station pulled away from Flordon and fortunately its speed was still low when it collided with a ballast wagon..' No one was seriously injured but the engine, tender and luggage van were derailed.[8]

Chappel viaduct.

Further accidents occurred as the network expanded although there were no fatalities between 1846 and 1851. But the dangerous nature of working on the railways as this time can be seen from this report in the *Ipswich Journal* in 1846:

> On Saturday last as John Kent, a porter in the goods department at the

Eastern Union station, was in the act of coupling the engine to an empty train, he inadvertently dropped his hand from the block on the buffer rod whilst the engine was backing in and crushed it in a frightful manner. Amputation was resorted to within half an hour.[9]

Reputation of Eastern Counties

Despite this expansion, it had become apparent the infrastructure needed to sustain the railways in the region was not in place. There was an urgent need for more locomotives, maintenance depots, goods sheds and coal depots. In the summer of 1845, there had already been two fatalities caused by the unsuitability of wheels on the engine. The following year, the local Norwich newspapers had begun a campaign against the poor state of the railway system. It was becoming clear that many railways were being poorly managed. There was also increasing criticism of the way in which George Hudson was operating; his only concern being profit. But there was also evidence that the locomotives needed to be improved.

Despite the professional management and engineering leadership of Peter Bruff, the line continued to suffer from poor industrial relations, unskilled workers and lack of good rolling stock. Although, compared with other forms of employment, railway workers were reasonably well paid and had secure employment, attempts to reduce wages and poor management led to unrest, and in 1850 there was a major attempt at a railway strike on the Eastern Counties. In August 1850 178 railwaymen handed in their notices demanding that the superintendent of the line be sacked. But rather than recognise they had a problem, the company decided to blacklist these workers and found replacements from other railways or locally unemployed men.

Another example of poor management came when direct trains started from London to Yarmouth via Cambridge. There was a lack of preparation and consideration of the impact of the sudden arrival of large numbers of people on the east coast from London. Trains were overcrowded and there had been no forethought as to where people would eat or stay when in Yarmouth. One train alone had 53 carriages carrying 2,000 passengers with no opportunity for refreshments during the six hour journey.

Correspondence in the *Ipswich Journal* in 1851 complained about the unruly nature of passengers on these overcrowded trains, particularly on the special cheap excursions from London to Ipswich on Sundays. Similar complaints about excursion trains on Sundays were made in the *Essex Standard*, throughout 1854, about large numbers of people arriving in Harwich causing a 'nuisance and disturbing' the local residents on the Sabbath.[10]

Creation of Great Eastern Railway

Although the Eastern Counties Railway had a poor reputation, it was much more powerful and influential than its competitor the Eastern Union. The Eastern Counties had the prime base of Norwich and, by 1854, merger between the two became inevitable. The gradual absorption of other smaller railway companies during the 1850s led, in 1862, to the creation of the Great Eastern Railway (GER). For the first time there was a railway system under one ownership and management that linked London, Cambridge, Ipswich, Norwich and Yarmouth. The only major routes that remained outside of this system were the lines that linked Norwich with the Midlands, with Melton Constable as its hub, and these were run by the Midland and Great Northern. The tensions between the GER and M&GN remained for many years although they did agree on joint ownership of lines linking East Anglia to Spalding and Lincoln. The importance of this link up was considerable. Not only did it enable trains to run across England from east to west, it also enabled trains to run direct from the Midlands and the North through to Harwich which was becoming an important port and gateway to the continent.

A further major development in the growth of the GER was the creation of a new and more central London terminus at Liverpool Street. This opened in 1874 and was part of several other GER initiatives. In 1870 it ended the supplement fare for faster or 'express trains'. In 1872 it was the first company to admit third class passengers to all trains, and subsequently, in 1891, within the exclusive precincts of a dining car. 1893 saw the abolition of second class on all but the continental boat trains and London suburban trains.

The creation of Liverpool Street station also enabled the expansion of the GER network in the latter decades of the 19th century. The labour force grew from about 20,000 in the late 1880s to about 25,000 by the turn of the century.[11] Howlett's study on the GER workforce in the late 19th century showed that the majority of the workers entered the company as either lads or porters, thereby unskilled at the point of entry.[12] His study showed that there was a clear internal labour market within the company at that time which shows that not all of the newly employed workers stayed in the company and developed skills. This evidence shows the complex nature of the workforce at this time and, despite the value workers put on having a secure job, there were other factors that mitigated against people staying within the GER.

Poor Reputation of Great Eastern Railway and conditions for railway workers

Although the merger into the GER helped to improve the infrastructure of the region's railways, there were still major problems with shortage of locomotives, poor timekeeping and increased industrial unrest.

A pamphleteer in 1860, although prior to the formation of the GER, wrote:

> Notoriously there is no railway system in the Empire so badly worked as the Eastern Counties. There is no system on which the passenger trains are so few or irregular; none on which the rates for Passengers and Goods are so excessive: and few, if any, where accidents are plentiful.[13]

Stories of minor crimes on the lines and at the stations were rife. Many of them concerned stealing goods from the freight wagons. Occasionally railway workers themselves were responsible, for example, in Norwich, James Clark was convicted for stealing cloth from a freight train.[14]

Working conditions were particularly difficult for those men who laid and repaired the track, the platelayers. In 1850, nine of them were killed near Brentwood. Serious accidents continued throughout that decade. One, in January 1854 following heavy snow, was a result of trains being on the wrong line. Unfortunately, the record did not improve in the following decades with serious accidents in 1866 near Ely, Kelvedon in 1872, and in 1874, near Norwich Thorpe station. This last accident is discussed further in chapter eight.

The railway workers had poor equipment to work with. Engines had no continuous brake system before the 1880s. In 1879, a train coming into Wells-next-the-Sea failed to break soon enough and ran into the station hitting the buffer stops. It appears the driver had been driving the train too fast coming into the station.

Railway workers were also vulnerable to victimisation if they aired any grievances. While, the GER settled a long running pay dispute by increasing wages of engine drivers, firemen and signalmen by two shillings a week in 1872, many still worked long hours. This was particularly a problem for signalmen who, because of the nature of their work, had long periods of inactivity followed by the need to suddenly change a number of points.

For the first forty years of the railway industry there were no trade unions. Only with the creation of the Amalgamated Society of Railway Servants (ASRS) in 1871 were the railway workers, in particular, in a position to have some support. One of the main issues railwaymen were concerned about was whether railway companies would give compensation to workers for injuries. What happened, in practice, was the creation of friendly societies to support widows of railway workers.

Despite the various problems with the various railway companies, the network expanded throughout East Anglia in the mid-19th century. What assisted their growth was undoubtedly the skill and vision of leading engineers like Peter Bruff, with the completion of the main line from Colchester to Norwich his greatest achievement.

Before looking in more detail at the legacy of Bruff's endeavours through the various lines in East Anglia, it is important to take stock of the transformative impact the railways had in the 19th century on local economies.

Notes

1 *Ross (2010).*

2 *Barney (2007).*

3 *Beaumont (2002) pp.130-133.*

4 *Moffat (1987).*

5 *Barney (2007).*

6 *Moffat (1987) p.41.*

7 *Hilton (1946) p.18.*

8 *Moffat (1987) p.156.*

9 *Ipswich Journal 19.9.1846, quoted in Gale (2015) p.68.*

10 *Major (2015) pp.141-142.*

11 *Howlett (2001) p.7.*

12 *Ibid.*

13 *Quoted in Gale (2015) p.16.*

14 *Miller (2013) p.48.*

Transforming The Rural Economy

Although the railways came late to East Anglia, they had a great effect on rural life in the towns and villages. Trains not only ensured mobility of people, but also provided a much quicker means of transport to move freight around than river or road. Railways, as already noted, also offered secure and relatively well-paid employment. Consequently, many agricultural labourers moved from the land to the railways. Railways also brought an end to mail being carried by stagecoach.

This chapter provides an overview of the impact of the railways on the rural economy and then looks at specific examples, such as the growing specialisation of particular crops and farm produce in particular areas. The chapter also examines the continual drift to urban areas and the consequent growth of major towns and cities.

Movement of Freight and Role of Railway Clerks

The first use of the railways for the transportation of freight commenced in 1846 and soon, not only was rail used for movement of local goods, but became the main means of moving coal around the region and providing access to markets for perishable goods. This was particularly important for a region like East Anglia, which had no coal or iron but did have plentiful agricultural produce and, with a long coastline, fishing. By the late 1840s, London was receiving over 70 tons of fresh fish a week from Yarmouth and Lowestoft via rail. From 1850s right up to 1970s, freight was much more important, and valuable, than passenger revenue.

Signalman in the late 19th century.

To support this growth in freight, infrastructure became more vital to success. For example, the rail routes in order to cope with increased traffic had to develop more advanced signalling technology, and the workers servicing this technology had to be well-trained and professional.

Larger stations in the region had a goods office for dealing with the receiving and dispatching of freight, however large or small. To support this service, stations had to employ railway clerks. They became an indispensable feature of larger railway stations. However, their life was not an easy one, having to be very precise in their work and to deal with a wide range of materials. It was a profession that, not surprisingly, had a high turnover of staff. They were often called upon to deal with disputes between companies regarding the loss or late arrival of goods, and at times, appearing as witnesses in cases involving stolen goods.[1] The railway clerks in many companies had a low status, 'practically slave labour'. An example of their status can be seen in this instruction given on the Midland and Great Northern Railway:

> The company will be sufficiently benevolent to provide a fire for the Clerical staff, each of whom should bring with him a daily lump of coal, to enable it to be lit.[2]

A particular problem in East Anglia was the transport of livestock with animals jumping out of open wagons or not being properly cared for whilst in transit.

Transformation of Agricultural Economy

The growth of the railways helped to transform the agriculturally based economy. The so-called prosperous era of High Farming (1850-1873) when loss of protection against foreign corn was countered by rationalisation and application of science to agriculture. The trend from arable to mixed farming quickened. There was also the movement of stock by rail from Scotland to Norfolk for fattening that helped.

The rural economies of East Anglia in the 19th century were not devoid of industries. Some of them were however serving just local needs, such as building materials with kilns and quarries, but others were directly related to specific agricultural produce, such as barley for brewing. East Anglia had a large number of breweries during this period and, as Alderton has shown, the growth and success of maltings became increasingly influenced by access to rail links, often with sidings from the site to the local lines.[3] Whilst Ipswich became a major centre for malting and brewing, there were also, by 1855, maltings centred in Southwold, Halesworth, Snape, Aldeburgh and Woodbridge.[4]

There is evidence that industrially based companies, upon seeing the opportunity of increased access to markets, moved their factories to be near rail links. One example was Colman's mustard factory in Norwich which in 1854 moved to a new site with access to the new rail links. Such factories not only benefited from easy access for transportation of its goods, the railways provided a quick and easy means of transporting coal, which was essential for power for their machines.

Railways offered relief in many ways. Their ability to check the "overwhelming evil" of the Poor Rates and the creation of employment was an obvious positive benefit to the economy of the region. They also ensured that moving produce and livestock at a much cheaper rate would become possible. Particularly important was the access to London markets. One consequence was that many Norfolk farmers now diversified their approach, rearing livestock alongside growing crops. The location of the region to London also helped. An example was the developing practice of sending Midland livestock into the county for fattening before dispatch to the London meat markets. The great advantage to be gained by the farmers was the elimination of the fourteen day drove from Norfolk, which usually served to reduce the animals to a wretched condition.

For some towns however there was a negative consequence of this transformation of the agricultural economy. One example was the decline of Kings Lynn as a port and market town. As Gordon has noted:

> Lynn, being without reserves of any kind, suffered far more than the vast majority of towns of commensurate size and importance from the introduction of the railway system at large. Armes wrote in 1852 that "nothing, that I am aware of, has occurred to affect the naturally favourable position of Lynn but the introduction of the railway system", (quoted in Gordon p.541) and Thew, looking back from 1890 over the events of the previous fifty-two years, held that: the decline and almost total extinction of the nautical business to which Lynn owed its prosperity during several centuries was caused by the introduction of the railway system diverting the course of traffic into new routes.[5]

But for others, such as those on the Suffolk and Essex coast, including Southwold, Aldeburgh, Felixstowe and Maldon, there were now rail links to the major markets. This led to some specialisations, such as the growing of green peas in the Maldon area. In 1902, over eleven thousand tons of peas were dispatched in one season. Joby notes 'In one single day some three hundred trucks of peas were received at Bishopsgate goods depot' for dispatching around London.[6]

Above all the growth of railways resulted in people throughout the country, and particularly in the large towns and cities, having access to fresh produce.

By end of the 19th century, people in London would have access to East Anglian fruit, bloaters and kippers from Yarmouth and fish from Lowestoft. Cod and chips now became an important part of the British diet.

Although farming and fishing prospered from increased access to markets, improvements in marine transport and usage of first canning, and then refrigeration, began to have their impact by the end of the 19th century. Corn, meat and dairy could be imported not only from Europe but also from America and Australia.

Throughout the 19th and well into the 20th century, all aspects of urban and rural economies relied on one essential fuel, coal. Railways became the means for transporting coal from the Midlands and the North to the eastern counties. A key centre for organising this transport was March which developed into one of the largest marshalling yards in Europe.

Increased Migration

A noticeable result of these changes in the late 19th and well into the 20th century was the gradual decline in the rural population of Norfolk, Suffolk and Essex. The railways played an important role in this movement from rural to urban areas. As a result of urbanisation and concentration of industries, villages declined and towns grew. Ipswich, for example, grew from 25,264 in 1841 to over 120,447 a century later.

However, having railway stations did not always guarantee high population growth. Wood's study of Norfolk migration in the 19th century shows that the railways not only had a beneficial effect on Norwich, Yarmouth and Lynn, but also on the whole county. Wood also shows that while the railways increased migration to London, many of the poorer families could not have afforded the rail fare. They relied on steam ships from Yarmouth or walking all the way on foot. He suggests that the effect of the 'railway was primarily psychological':

> The novelty of the railway must have been a factor in how migrants thought about their move. ... the more enterprising of its younger residents increasingly seeing Norfolk as a backwater from which to escape, the railway symbolising the new life that they desired. If they could not afford the price of a ticket to travel down to London the first time, many must have thought that after making, if not a fortune, a better living in the capital, they would be able to use the railway to visit their relatives and friends back home in Norfolk and, perhaps, pay for them to come down to stay.[7]

Railways also provided opportunities for families to move from one part of the UK to another. There is evidence that from the late 19th century, and even up to the mid-20th century, of farming families moving from Scotland to East Anglia to increase their prospects. One of these was the Wilson family who moved from Strathaven, in Lanarkshire, to Dallinghoo, in Suffolk, in 1919. Mr. Wilson frequently returned to Scotland to bring down dairy cattle where they could graze on marshland around Aldeburgh.[8]

Emergence of Rural Lines

A railway map of East Anglia shows, as well as the main lines from the major conurbations (*Map 1 p.18*), a series of small lines to coastal ports and holiday resorts. Some of these are discussed in the next chapter. But what is also evident are a series of inter-linking lines across rural Norfolk which were part of the Midland and Great Northern Railway (*Map 2*). They also acted as connecting towns in the county with the Midlands and the North. The epicentre of this railway, Melton Constable, is discussed in detail in a later chapter.

Many of these branch lines were built in the late 19th century to maximise quick connections for agricultural produce to the markets in London and the main cities. However not all new railways were developed as a response to economic need. Some, such as the Mid-Suffolk and the Kelvedon to Tollesbury lines,

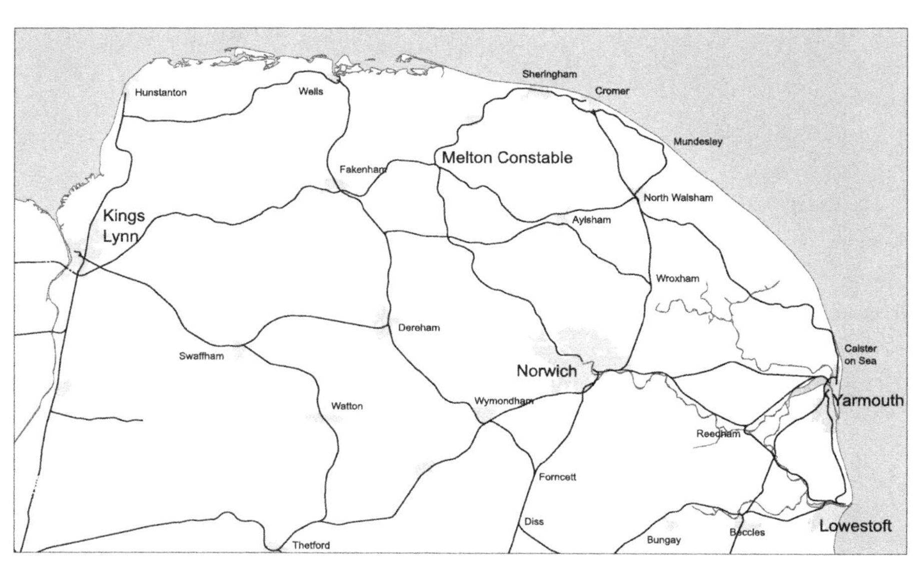

Map 2. Norfolk railway lines in the late 19th century, showing the profusion of lines.

opened at the turn of the century to exploit potential economic opportunities.[9] The Kelvedon to Tollesbury line or 'Crab and Winkle', as it became affectionately known, ended with a pier. The hope was to develop a port and holiday resort from scratch. Such lines rarely prospered and it closed during the inter-war years.

What also began to influence the economy of the East Anglia was the ease of access to London and the expansion of commuter land, with middle and upper classes moving out to leafy suburbs like Chingford and Ongar, then further still to Brentwood, Shenfield and Chelmsford.

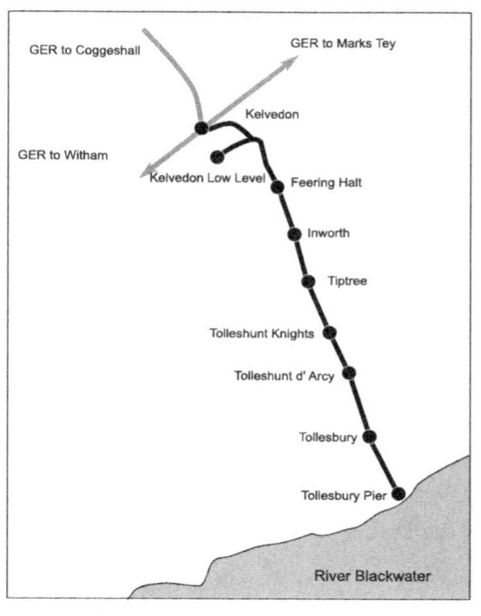

Map 3. The Kelvedon and Tollesbury Light Railway.

The railways were a major driver for changes in the nature of employment patterns and the economy of East Anglia. The region benefited from having quicker and easier access to main markets for its agricultural and fishing produce. But what the railways also provided were opportunities for the movement of peoples and communities into East Anglia and within the region from rural to urban areas.

Notes

1 *Gale (2015) p.27.*

2 *Back (2019) p.38-41.*

3 *Alderton (2005).*

4 *MacDonald (2017) p.23.*

5 *quoted in Gordon (1964) p.541.*

6 *Joby (1987) p.71.*

7 *Woods (2014).*

8 *Freestone and Smith (1998) p.94).*

9 *Stapleton(1962), House (2013).*

Growth of Tourism and Seaside Towns

Railways provided an opportunity to transform many people's leisure time. With reductions in working hours and, later, the introduction of holiday pay, seaside holidays became possible for working class people as well as the rich and middle class.

East Anglia, because of its proximity to London and many Midlands industrial centres, was ideally placed to respond to this growth. Around the coastlines of Norfolk, Suffolk and Essex were many villages and small towns that were ideal for holiday makers. Railway companies were conscious of this and put a great deal of effort to ensure that places such as Hunstanton, Wells, Sheringham, Cromer, Yarmouth, Lowestoft, Southwold, Aldeburgh, Felixstowe, Dovercourt, Clacton, Walton and Brightlingsea all had railway connections. Whilst a number of these embryo resorts did not survive, the railway map at the end of the 19th century shows the extent to which the railways were being geared towards tourism and the coast.

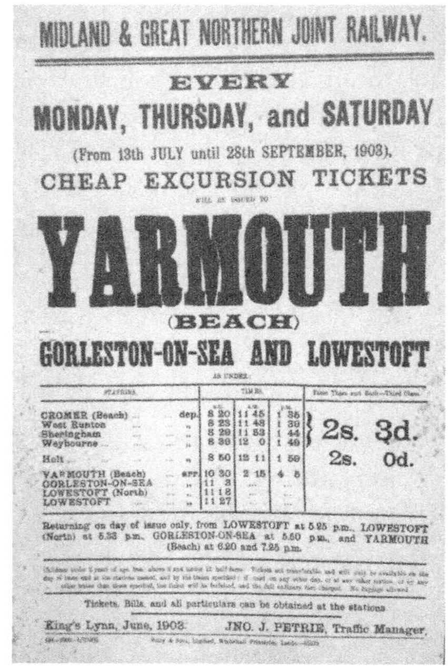

A 1903 M&GN poster advertising cheap excursion tickets to the east coast resorts.

An important reason for the popularity of these east coast resorts, particularly for people from the London area, was their ease of access for short breaks. An example of this can be seen over the August Bank holiday of 1899 when over 40,000 tickets were sold in a single day and this, of course, does not account for those returning from short breaks.

For many people at the end of the 19th century and into the first decade of the 20th, the bicycle had become a popular means of transport. East Anglia provided an ideal landscape for cycling, relatively flat land and plenty of railway stations to get on and off at with your bike. Ticket records for one day at Liverpool Street showed 1300 bikes on trains.

The importance of Bank Holidays, providing millions of people with the opportunity to travel by train for the day or the weekend to coastal resorts, grew right up to the outbreak of war in 1939. For example, in that year, over 14,000 people travelled from Norwich Thorpe station on Whit Monday and between 20,000 and 25,000 on the August Bank Holiday Monday. The most popular destination being Great Yarmouth.[1]

The following chapter will look in more depth at one of these towns, Lowestoft, but in this chapter the aim is to give some examples or stories of what life was like working and using these railways. The chapter consciously looks at two areas where the lines have survived, Cromer and Clacton with Walton, and three that have closed, Mundesley in Norfolk, and Southwold and Aldeburgh in Suffolk.

Cromer

At a mid-point along the north Norfolk coast is Cromer. This 19th century fishing village became a popular holiday resort. The opening of a railway to the town in 1877 was further helped by the writings of the travel journalist Clement Scott and its popularity in the late 19th century meant that, at one stage, it had three different stations (Cromer High, Beach and Links Halt). Cromer became a popular destination for Victorians, and hotels and guest houses soon opened up.

Trains were able to come via two routes to the seaside town, one via Cambridge and the other via Ipswich. By the end of the 19th century, the fashionability of the town could be seen by the time it took to arrive at Cromer from London. By-passing Norwich, trains arrived just under three hours from leaving the capital. Like other resorts, Cromer's growth in popularity was aided by royal patronage, following a visit to the resort in 1877 by the Princess of Wales and Duke and Duchess of York.

By the end of the century, Cromer was fast becoming a stylish resort and as the *Railway Magazine* remarked in 1898, this was in no small part due to the railway and the introduction of the *Cromer Express* two years earlier:

> ...great as are its natural advantages it would still probably 'blush unseen and waste its sweetness in the desert air' but for the aid and encouragement given to it by the spiritual policy pursued by the Great Eastern.[2]

In the years up to the outbreak of war in 1914, the *Cromer Express*, later renamed the *Norfolk Coast Express*, became known for arriving at its destination in a slightly faster time than its previous record. The service was withdrawn on the outbreak of war and although Cromer could be reached directly between the

Queen Alexandra is escorted to Cromer High station after staying with Lord Hillingdon in 1902.

wars, these services were not as fast, and the Express name was withdrawn.

Following a reduction in traffic caused by Cromer's declining popularity as a holiday destination after World War II, and the closure of many Norfolk railway lines in the 1950s, a decision was made to concentrate all passenger traffic into a single station. Although Cromer High had far better facilities, it was inconveniently situated on the edge of the town. Therefore, all passenger services were diverted into Cromer Beach (renamed Cromer). Following the growth of the town as a commuter town to Norwich, a new station called Roughton Road opened in 1985, near the site of the former Cromer High.

Cromer continued to attract tourists in the post-World War Two period. Holiday trains arrived from the Midlands, the North and London direct to the town. Well into the 1950s, there was the daily *Broadsman* from London to Cromer which took three and half hours. Even with the closure of lines beyond Sheringham to Melton Constable and to Mundesley to the east, the station remained popular. It continues to be a well liked destination today, particularly for day trippers. Around the town and adjacent communities there remains a large number of caravans and other forms of holiday accommodation. However, much of the station's former importance can no longer be seen today. It had an extensive goods yard but all freight traffic ceased in 1969. The yard was replaced by a large supermarket.

Mundesley

This picturesque village on the North Norfolk coast opened its railway station in 1893 on the line from North Walsham to Cromer. It was a grand station with sufficient facilities to handle large numbers of passengers. There were high hopes that the resort could become another Cromer. Within a space of a few years of its opening, three hotels were built on the seafront close to the station. A holiday camp was also opened in the village in 1930. Various attempts were made to promote Mundesley as a holiday destination. The *Norfolk Coast Express*, from 1906, had sections to Mundesley as well as Sheringham and Cromer.

During the first decade of the 20th century, Mundesley was a very busy station with seventeen trains each way daily from North Walsham. This high volume was in part due to competition between the Great Eastern with the M & GN companies.

In an attempt to get more passengers, a 'camping coach' was based in the bay platform for the summer seasons in 1938 and 1939. These coaches were returned in 1952 and in 1961 and were increased from four to six carriages.

It was a resort I knew well from my childhood as I had a great aunt and uncle living at nearby Paston and we often went there for the day from Melton Constable. What I remember is a fabulous sandy beach but the place had few amenities for holidaymakers compared to nearby Cromer and Sheringham or Great Yarmouth. By the time I went there as a child, the railway was faced with closure.

Without passengers all year round, the line to Mundesley was doomed particularly as the population of the village did not grow significantly in the early decades of the 20th century. In the post-war period, with the growth of

Mundesley railway station in 1902, looking east with the village in the background.

road transport, the Cromer-Mundesley line was an inevitable casualty with the line closing in 1953. It was perhaps surprising that the rest of the line to North Walsham stayed open but when it came to Beeching's proposals it became an easy route to close. The last trains from North Walsham to Mundesley ran in December 1964.

Southwold

Although an important Suffolk coastal port and town in the 19th century, Southwold was at first neglected by the railway entrepreneurs. Eventually, as a result of lobbying from local business people, a branch was constructed from nearby Halesworth from the Ipswich to Lowestoft line to Southwold via nearby Walberswick. Finances being tight, a narrow gauge line, 3 feet in width, was built, opening for passengers in 1879. At first the line was popular. In 1880, over 65,000 people travelled on it. But it continued to suffer from mishaps with flooding in 1882, a fatal accident in 1883 and various criminal activity. Despite these, by 1900 the line carried over 100,000 passengers, plus large quantities of minerals and other goods.[3] The freight traffic had been helped by the development of a small sidings and rails down to the quayside for the fishing boats that used the Blyth estuary just south of the main town.

Southwold Railway's Arthur Edgar Wright pictured c.1910. The guard on the first train on the railway's opening day in 1879, he served until retirement in 1914.

The station being situated just outside the town did not help. Nor did the location of the halt at Walberswick, which was even further away from the centre of the village. The trains had a charming, almost toytown, look about them. The locomotives were small, well-kept, with a blue livery hauling just a couple of maroon coaches plus some goods wagons and guard's van.

The quaintness and informality of the line can be seen from the following account:

> I well remember a delay in Walberswick station one morning when the engine sounded its whistle but it did not leave the station, and on looking out of the window I saw the Guard climb to the top of the bank and look towards the village, then signal the driver to proceed. After a short

distance the train stopped with a jerk, as a man was seen running towards the station, and as soon as he was safely on board the train made up for lost time. This passenger turned out to be a regular who had over slept on that particular morning.[4]

Freight never became that important to the line although it was used for carrying fish from the port to London. Unusually, coal came into the port by steamer and was then carried in from the town to adjacent communities by rail.

It was hoped that the line would help to encourage holiday-makers to the town which had excellent amenities, including a good beach. There is some evidence that in the late 19th century and first decade of the 20th the line was popular particularly at August Bank holiday times. For example, on one day in 1899, over 400 return tickets were issued to Southwold from nearby Halesworth.

But apart from these special days, the line was not well used. The trains were slow and uncomfortable and were subject to ridicule by local cartoonists. The official maximum speed on the line was sixteen miles per hour. Passengers mounted the coaches at either end and sat on long benches facing each other. Attempts were made to widen the gauge to standard, which would result in faster trains and would have made through services to Ipswich and beyond possible. There was also a plan to build a line northwards to Lowestoft. But neither of these proposals came to anything.

Southwold had a reputation as a 'higher-class' resort and never succeeded

Southwold railwaymen: F.C.Moore, Fireman (on footplate); F.(Putter) Collett, Driver (in the locomotive.

in developing the mass tourism of other east coast towns. Attempts were made with cheap excursion tickets in 1923 and 1924. But, as Paye has noted, it only attracted more well-to-do families from London:

> For a number of years before and after World War One well-healed London city businessmen rented houses at seaside resorts during the summer season, moving their families and servants to the coast so that they could enjoy the sea air away from the metropolis.[5]

The First World War saw the line begin to go into decline. Gone were holidaymakers and freight traffic virtually disappeared.

After the war, at first passenger numbers, whilst not reaching their pre-war level, were still substantial. Memories of people who used the line during this period highlight its old-fashioned qualities, spartan carriages and the good humour of the staff. But it was the introduction of a bus service and the failure to re-invest in the line, and its rolling stock in particular, that resulted in a significant reduction in passenger travel. As most of the stations were not in the middle of the communities, the railway was always going to lose out to the buses who could drop passengers close to where they lived. Attempts were made to address the competition, including reduced fare tickets and special excursions, which saw a temporary increase in use during 1927. Railway staff had already been forced to take several wage cuts during the 1920s in an attempt to reduce costs. But by now motor buses, that could do the distance to Halesworth much faster than the train won the battle and it was no surprise that the line closed in 1929. Thirty men were now without employment, and for some of them, the years that followed were very difficult given the economic depression and lack of alternative work.

Despite the closure of the line, nearly a century ago, there is still interest in the Southwold Railway. Remnants of the former line can still be seen at Walberswick, and there is an active heritage trust company which is developing a visitor centre with plans to rebuild the line.[6]

Aldeburgh

Although Aldeburgh is today an important seaside resort, this was the initial motivation for the development and construction of a line—a branch off the Ipswich to Lowestoft line from Saxmundham. Before the coming of railways there was a well-established engineering works at Leiston, a few miles inland from Aldeburgh, and the Garratt family, who owned the works, were keen to support and sponsor a railway line that would enable easier movement of their goods. The line opened in 1860. At first, freight was the main generator of income, not only from the engineering works, but also, agricultural produce and fish.

At first there were five trains each way every day between Aldeburgh and Saxmundham. These increased after the First World War to eight services. There were also attempts, between the wars, to develop direct services from Aldeburgh to London.

The line had a further boost with the growth of Thorpeness in the first decade of the 20th century. The development of this village, the brainchild of Glencairn Stuart Ogilvie, as a fantasy holiday settlement with half-timbered houses, a mere, golf courses and swimming pools was planned to boost the local economy and the railway. A station was therefore opened to serve this settlement in 1914 but it does not appear to have succeeded.

In contrast, Aldeburgh's popularity as a holiday destination grew and from 1906 there were through trains to the town from London. The town was even included as a destination on the *Eastern Belle Pullman*. This service offered high speed trains to different East Anglian resorts on selected days with elite Pullman coaches. A summer service continued until the outbreak of war in 1939. In the post-war period, despite the introduction of the world famous Aldeburgh music festival, the railway suffered like many similar lines in East Anglia. As a holiday resort, it still tended to cater for the middle and upper classes and could not compete with the greater holiday traffic now going to more popular resorts along the coastline, such as Great Yarmouth and Clacton.

Local businesses, particularly the Garratt's engineering works, had incentivised the development of the line. But, despite it being used by this firm and others, goods traffic gradually declined and the freight service was withdrawn in 1959. Passenger services ceased in 1966 as part of the Beeching cuts.

This was not the end of the line because, with the construction of the Sizewell nuclear power station near Leiston, British Railways, with support from the nuclear power industry decided to keep the line open to Leiston for the transportation of nuclear flask containers. The track is still there today and there are still occasional trains carrying nuclear material from Leiston. It is hoped that one day this line might again be used for passengers. Remnants

The Sizewell terminus.

of the line on to Aldeburgh can still be seen near Thorpeness.

Clacton and Walton-on-the-Naze

Walton, on the north east Essex coast near Frinton, was already known as a holiday destination by the time the railway came to the town. By 1830, for example, it already had a pier and a hotel. While working on the Ipswich line in 1855, Peter Bruff bought a house, Burnt House Farm, in Walton. He began to work on developing Walton as a recognised seaside resort, his main objective being the opening of a branch line from Colchester. This was accomplished in 1867 with a line from Colchester via Wivenhoe and Thorpe-le-Soken. Another line to nearby Brightlingsea had opened the previous year. By the end of the 1870s, Walton was on the way to becoming a popular seaside resort although its distance from London meant that it was unlikely to attract as many day visitors as Southend.[7]

In 1871 Peter Bruff, the steamboat owner William Jackson and a group of businessmen started to look further afield, and the nearby villages of Great and Little Clacton, where there was an excellent beach, provided an opportunity for another resort. A pier and hotel were built and the town of Clacton-on-Sea was officially incorporated in 1872. Ten years later the railway came with a spur from Thorpe-le-Soken to Clacton-on-Sea.

At first the line was only a single track and this hindered the number of trains that could use the line. But this was gradually addressed, and by 1889 there were six trains a day in each direction between Colchester, Clacton and Walton, with the train being divided into two parts at Thorpe-le-Soken. By the turn of the century the train service had become regular enough for Clacton and Walton to be within reach of London for daily commuters.

Bruff was largely responsible for the development of Clacton as a seaside town. On his arrival in 1864, Bruff made a private deal to buy 50 acres in the central part of the town for around £10,000. The land centred on the area each side of the current pier and back into the town centre. In approximately 1870, work began on the seaside resort of Clacton-on-Sea. The *Times* in 1871 wrote:

> That being an entirely new creation and not the adaptation of an existing town, none of the evils inseparable from the old watering holes will be allowed to exist in it. There will be no slums, nor any object that can offend the eye.[8]

When the pier opened, the town truly began to grow.

His later constructions in the town included: the Royal Hotel in 1872, a public hall in Pier Avenue, which was destroyed by a fire in 1939, and the creation of the town centre. There is now a hospital ward and a residential road named in Bruff's memory.

Clacton grew into the largest seaside resort between Southend-on-Sea and Great Yarmouth, with some 10,000 residents by 1914 and around 20,000 by 1939. Due to its accessibility from the East End of London and the Essex suburbs, Clacton, like Southend, predominantly catered for working-class and lower-middle-class holidaymakers. In 1920, conscious of the growing popularity of Clacton and Walton, more holiday excursion trains were introduced from London including a Sunday Pullman class train called the *Clacton Belle*, later renamed the *Eastern Belle*.

The popularity of Clacton as a holiday resort in the inter-war period was helped by the building of a Butlin's holiday camp in the town and the introduction of a statutory week's holiday pay in 1938. For example, on the eve of the outbreak of war in 1939 on the August Bank Holiday weekend, nearly 35,000 people travelled to Clacton by train. Most of them were day trippers from London.

The greatest demand came in the 1950s and 1960s. One summer Saturday in 1951, between 8.00 and 13.10, saw sixteen departures for Clacton including

Malcolm Root's evocative painting of the Butlin Express arriving at Clacton.

three non-stop trains.[9] On Saturdays and Sundays in the 1950s, up to 10,000 people could be seen queuing to get into the station at Clacton to get on trains back to London and stops in-between. The Colchester to Clacton and Walton services were electrified for local services in 1959 and, from 1962, with through electric services to London.

By the end of the 1970s, interest in resorts like Clacton was declining with holidays abroad gaining momentum. In 1983 an era ended with the closure of the Butlins' holiday camp.

Today the line, with an excellent service to London, has become a commuter base for London. Caton, in his volume on train travel around the UK, remarks:

> With four platforms and its original large buildings, Clacton station looks as if it should be served by more than the hourly London trains which are the only off-peak activity. Gone are the days of holiday trains arriving from across the country, although on sunny weekends there are still a good number of day trippers. With an eighty-six-minute journey to London (five minutes quicker than 1976), commuters are now the line's main users.[10]

These examples demonstrate the interrelationship between the growth and, in some areas, decline of tourism in East Anglia with the railways. The railways provided a quick and easy access from the main cities to fine beaches and a dry and warm climate. Although some of these resorts no longer have the popularity they once had, one can still find places, like Cromer, having thousands of visitors on a summer's day.

Notes

1 *Brown (1980) p.126.*

2 *Whitechurch (1898).*

3 *Lee, Taylor and Shorland-Hall (2019).*

4 *Jenkins (2012) p.18.*

5 *Paye (2018) p.176.*

6 *https://www.southwoldrailway.co.uk*

7 *Phillips (1989) p.10.*

8 *quoted in https://prabook.com/web/peter.bruff/1953594*

9 *Dawes (2019).*

10 *Caton (2013) p.124.*

Lowestoft: The Most Easterly Railway Station

Lowestoft is another town with strong family connections. It's where my father was born and where many of his family and therefore some of my aunts, uncles and cousins still reside. It is a place I most fondly remember for my summer holidays as a child. Following a week in North Norfolk, we then went to Lowestoft for a week. I found it a great place for summer holidays with good beaches, amazing fish including the local speciality of 'bloaters' and a good base for excursions to nearby holiday resorts such as Yarmouth and Gorleston.

The barquentine J.S.Sterry is towed through the Lowestoft swing bridge at the turn of the 20th century.

This chapter outlines the development and history of the influence and importance of the railway to Lowestoft. It includes the role of Samuel Morton Peto, who is often seen as the founder of modern day Lowestoft. The chapter covers Lowestoft's growth not only as a port but as a holiday resort, and its economic decline, particularly since the 1970s.

Perhaps Lowestoft is a showcase for a number of key themes in the development of railways in East Anglia. Firstly, it demonstrates how the railway can transform a town into a holiday resort by becoming accessible by rail to London and many major conurbations in the Midlands. Secondly, it provided the opportunity for local fish produce to be on the dinner tables in London the same day as being caught. Thirdly, and because of these developments, the railways meant a rapid expansion from this small seaside village into a major national port.

As M. White has commented:

> From the middle of the 19th century, the railway at Lowestoft became the driving force for the development of the town, and provided a vital service to townspeople, visitors, business, the port and industry.[1]

Few towns of comparative size could match railway organisation, structure, number of lines and stations within the town boundary. The main station, Lowestoft Central, served three different routes and there were, at one time, another station (Lowestoft North) and a myriad of lines servicing the docks and nearby factories. The harbour was, from the mid-19th century, until 1963 run by the railway company.

Origins and Early Development of the Railway in the Town

Before the coming of the railway, Lowestoft was a small fishing community to the north of a shingle bank and Lake Lothing dividing it from Kirkley. It relied upon the sea and waterways for transportation of goods but there were no facilities for handling larger boats. With no harbour, the coming of the railways therefore transformed transport and movements of people and goods to and from the town. The community had always been under the shadow of its near neighbour and important fishing port in Great Yarmouth.

Lowestoft had already attracted the interest of businessmen in the early 1800s who were seeking a new outlet for cargo from Norwich as Yarmouth had high port tolls. Whilst the course of the Waveney river flowed into Lake Lothing near Lowestoft, access to the sea had to be constructed across the shingle bank to the sea. This opened in 1831. Lowestoft had a potentially valuable inner harbour and this gave the prospect of ships sailing direct from London to Norwich via the town.

However, this prospect was called into question a decade later, as ships became larger and the navigation more difficult. In May 1844 the railway between Yarmouth and Norwich had opened. Despite the efforts of a consortium of Lowestoft and Norwich businessmen to try and save the harbour, it was left to a increasingly influential businessman, Samuel Morton Peto, to save both the harbour and the town. He had already played an important role in the construction of the railway line from Yarmouth to Norwich with his cousin Grissell, and had also purchased a major property in the edge of Lowestoft, Somerleyton Hall.

Influence of Samuel Peto

Peto was already a successful businessman with a strong nonconformist work ethic and, typical of many 19th century businessmen, combined capitalist ventures with politics, becoming an MP (1847). He was involved in a number of railway ventures, including building of lines and track on the Great Western under Brunel and in and around London.

Peto has been regarded as the man who, more than any other, was responsible for the development of Lowestoft. His vision of both a holiday resort and a fishing port meant that Lowestoft became in the 19th century transformed from a small fishing community into a major tourist and fishing centre. This was due to his role in helping to construct the harbour in and around the town and the construction of railways that linked to lines to major towns and cities in the rest of East Anglia and to London.

Samuel Morton Peto

The start of this expansion began at a meeting at the Town Hall in Lowestoft in March 1843 where Peto outlined his plans. Building a railway, he said would ensure fresh fish, with the help of packed ice, could be on the dinner table the same day in London or Manchester. He also wanted the town to become a holiday resort and to further this ambition he had within six years ensured the building of the Royal Hotel and a series of houses close to the sea. He saw that for Lowestoft to be an important port, its harbours needed to be developed. He oversaw the construction of an inner and outer harbour that enabled fish to be easily offloaded from boats to either river barges and sent up to Norwich or to the emerging infrastructure of railway lines.

In 1845 the Lowestoft Railway and Harbour Company was formed, with the aim of building a railway line to Norwich and also the development of a harbour with rail lines to a new docks.

The following year, the construction of the railway began. In 1847, the first train, a goods train, ran from Lowestoft to Reedham. Peto subcontracted the building of the line to the engineers Robert Stephenson and George Bidder, while he built the harbour. Once the harbour and railway were completed in 1847, the town developed as a major centre for goods traffic, particularly with fish, timber and cattle.

Peto introduced a second railway line to Lowestoft when he connected it to East Suffolk in 1859 with a link at Oulton Broad. The status in which Peto was seen at this time can be seen in this song by a William Day, sung at the formal opening of the East Suffolk line at Lowestoft, which included the following phrases:

> 'A work for which we owe him much' and 'we may show our thanks as such as grateful men display...' and let this festive hall resound, Sir Morton Peto's name.[2]

However, this glowing tribute to Peto needs to be tempered by some criticisms from members of his workforce. Whilst he was known to be a benevolent employer, helping workers with sickness benefit, housing and encouraging teetotalism, he also had a reputation for being authoritarian. He was certainly opposed to any form of trade union activity but recognised the value of having a contented workforce. One of the things he did do at Lowestoft during the construction of the railway was to set up evening classes for the navvies. He was a very religious person and became MP for Norwich from 1847 to 1854 and later for Finsbury in London. Although his reputation became tarnished by later ventures, there is no doubt that his name is synonymous with the growth of Lowestoft as a town and it was due to his vision that it became for a century at least a successful port and also popular holiday resort.

Lowestoft Station

The initial railway station in Lowestoft, which opened in 1847, was some way from the main town. It had only two platforms, but with Peto's plans for the town to be a hub with links not only to Norwich and Yarmouth but also south to Ipswich, a new and more central terminus was built in 1855 by the Lucas Brothers, a nationally well-known company of builders. It was built in the Italianate style with the main buildings arranged in a L shape with booking and parcels office, refreshment rooms and bookstall. There was an impressive and lengthy roof over the platforms and concourse area, although nothing remains of its roof and surrounding structures today. I can remember it as a fine building and a fitting statement for the town.

Early train services were small scale with three trains a day to Norwich taking up to 90 minutes. In 1863 the first direct services to London began, taking 3¼ hours to complete the journey. The 1883 timetable shows eight stopping trains each way between Ipswich, Lowestoft and Yarmouth, with two or three services a day from London.

The importance of Lowestoft station can be seen in the growth of sidings, locomotive sheds and ancillary facilities in the late 19th and early 20th century.

An engraving of Lowestoft Railway Station, dating from 1855 showing the Italianate style of architecture so beloved of its creator, Samuel Morton Peto.

Lowestoft's railway sidings in 1980. A class 03 0-6-0 diesel shunting locomotive (no 03370) in the goods sidings besides the station. At this time some coal traffic was still handled in these sidings. The vans are for the delivery of parcels brought in by rail.

Locomotives require access to ready-made water supplies and for many years this was obtained from a reservoir north of the line, which was fed by a series of pipes from nearby springs.

Growth of the Town as a Port

With the arrival of the railway, Lowestoft's population doubled in sixteen years to reach 10,000 and by the end of the century it had increased to 36,000. Under the leadership of Peto, construction began in 1849 of the esplanade following the construction and enlargement of the Outer Harbour by building new North and South piers, a new trawl basin and fish market for 700 boats.

The port of Lowestoft grew rapidly and by the turn of the century over 50,000 tons of fish were landed annually. In 1866, a harbour railway line was built so that fish could be loaded directly on to railway trucks. In 1883 a new Herring basin, later to be known as Waveney Dock, was constructed. Another dock, Hamilton, was constructed in 1903.

Great Eastern Railway (GER) developed a monopoly over the commercial heart of the town owning the rail, quays, wharves and ships that operated out of the port. Lowestoft became second only to Grimsby in terms of number of men employed regularly in the fishing industry. By 1913, there were several hundred boats from Scotland using Lowestoft. The high point of the fishing industry came just before the outbreak of the First World War. Not only was the port very busy, but the number of connected industries and trades, such as sail and rope making and boat building ensured high employment.

Fish, Ferries and Seawater

As a result of the railway at Lowestoft fish became, from the middle of the 19th century, a staple of British diet. The most famous and obvious were cod and chips, but Suffolk specialities such as bloaters and kippers also became popular. The key season for herring fishing was the autumn and, to deal with the landing of vast quantities of fish at Lowestoft, several hundred fisher girls came from Scotland to gut, salt and barrel them. A curious bi-product of the herring season was the collection of seawater off the Lowestoft coast, which was put into large kegs and transported by train to London. This seawater was used for drinking, salt water baths and medical cures.

Another area that Peto had encouraged was the development of Lowestoft as a ferry port. A Denmark to Lowestoft cattle ferry service began in September 1850. Steamer services began to Rotterdam, Hamburg, Denmark, Norway and Sweden and there was also the growth of coastal trade. But Lowestoft was unable to compete with Harwich further down the coast, and as a consequence, the cattle trade was short lived.

Holiday Resort

What was more successful was the development of Lowestoft as a significant holiday resort. Whilst the town had been known in the early 19th century as a health resort for the wealthy, the coming of the railway opened up the town to the masses.

An Edwardian postcard view of Kirkley Cliff, Peto's resort development. Lowestoft harbour's South Pier is discernible on the skyline—its pavilion clearly seen.

In 1848 new accommodation for visitors was built. Peto was instrumental in promoting this expansion having purchased much of the waste heathland south of the new harbour.

The culmination of this first phase was the opening of Peto's Royal Hotel in 1849. Lowestoft's appeal as a holiday resort resulted in a major increase in rail traffic as families came from Norwich and surrounding areas for day trips to the seaside. In addition, from the summer of 1859, trains were split at Beccles for Lowestoft or Yarmouth, and visitors from London began to take holidays in the town.

An article in the *Illustrated London News* of 27 July 1850 shows the impact of the railway on the popularity of the town as a holiday destination:

> ...within the last two to three years, an extension of the Eastern Counties Railway has thrown (Lowestoft) open, and the population of the entire district, embracing an area of not less than 100 miles, have since kept flocking to see it in progressively increasing numbers...[3]

By 1889 there were ten trains each day between Lowestoft and Norwich. But it was not until the summer of 1904 that direct non-stop expresses were introduced from London. The traditional access to London was however by shuttle train connection out of the Yarmouth services at Beccles or by portions split and worked forward from there. Nine or ten passenger services to Norwich operated on weekdays and four on Sundays in 1905, the frequency increasing to twelve each way on weekdays by 1921. Throughout the earlier part of the 20th century, Lowestoft was a very busy rail terminus and port with substantial goods and sidings. Most of the goods and sidings with a freight only line operated on the south side of Lake Lothing. It became an important link to major factories and dealt with a wide range of goods and freight including wood, coal and bricks as well as agricultural produce, such as sugar beet. There were also the very important fishing products.

The success of Lowestoft as a holiday resort can be seen in 1919 when over 60,000 people used the station. Between the wars, the continued growth and popularity of the town was helped with the introduction of long-distance restaurant car express services in 1924, which ran from Liverpool, Manchester and Sheffield. Another boost to the town and holiday traffic was the construction of holiday camps in and near Lowestoft. *Holiday Camps Express* ran via Lowestoft to serve the holiday camps along the coast from 1934 to 1939 and then after the war until 1958. From the late 1940s to the late 1950s, Lowestoft station on Saturdays was a constant stream of arrivals and departures, at one stage every ten minutes. Many of the visitors to Lowestoft came from the surrounding countryside and other towns in Suffolk and Norfolk. A member of a branch of the Women's Institutes in Suffolk, in 1945, wrote in her diary:

> I started my week's holiday, jobbing at home. We all went by train to Lowestoft … Mr. Pinkney took us to Halesworth station and back for eight shillings.[4]

However, by early 1960s these trains had ended with the competition from the road and the beginning of overseas package holidays.

Lowestoft at its Peak

Between the wars saw Lowestoft at its peak with growing holiday traffic, a profitable fishing industry and ever-expanding goods traffic. The chief materials brought into Lowestoft included coal (from the East Midlands) bricks to Lowestoft North, pipes, glass, sheet metal plates, flour, beer, grain and wheel-rims to be exported to the Netherlands. Goods sent out from Lowestoft included canned foods, wood cases and fish to London and Bury St. Edmunds.

It is from this period and up until the late 1950s that the railway was regarded as one of the most important employers in the town. The railway was responsible for running the port and a sleeper depot. In 1914, a sleeper depot was opened on a reclaimed mud bank in Lake Lothing. It grew to cover thirteen acres and had a capacity of 450,000 sleepers. Following the closure of Melton Constable Works in 1936, the depot became a centre for the construction of many items such as fenceposts and building parts, which were sent all over the country. In addition, it incorporated a pre-cast sleeper depot which supplied over half of the Eastern Region with two or three special trains leaving it each week. In an average year, about 328,000 sleepers were dispatched with 10,600 tons of chairs and baseplates and many tons of small permanent way accessories. The activity continued until 1964.

The summer timetable of 1939 gives a good indication of the busy nature of Lowestoft as a rail terminus. There were seventeen trains each way per day. Local services to Norwich, Yarmouth and Ipswich were supplemented by long distance trains, particularly on Saturdays, to Newcastle, Leeds and Northampton.

Decline and Impact of War

By the outbreak of the Second World War there was evidence of some decline in aspects of the industries that influenced the railway. The fish traffic began to decline until there were only seasonal specials in addition to the fish vans on the daily return goods trip. The fall in income from fish traffic was only partially replaced by the development of holiday camps along the coast.

The war took a major toll on Lowestoft and its railway system. Its position on the east coast made it vulnerable to attack. The town was constantly bombed with 192 people losing their lives to air raids. It was the most heavily bombed town per head of population in the UK. As an east coast port, the town became a naval base. Trains had to be suddenly diverted or commissioned for war work such as constructing airfields.

Hewison in his autobiography of life as a railwayman included being based at Lowestoft for most of the war period. It shows the many sacrifices the railwaymen made for the war effort.[5] He noted that, despite poor engines and the constant threat of bombing raids, only once was a scheduled departure of an engine from Lowestoft shed delayed due to an air raid. Hewison also noticed the ruthless way in which the railway was run. Men were expected to get results with no fixed hours of duty for foremen. But what he noted was 'Lowestoft men were first class, drivers were masters of their calling and fitters were excellent'.

Before we discuss the details of the decline of the railways in and around Lowestoft after the war, it is important to note that into the 1950s British Railways was still one of the major employers in the town. It is estimated that up to a thousand people were employed in some form during this period. The town was still very popular in the 1950s and 1960s as a holiday resort. For example, in the 1950s up to 35 trains in each direction could be seen going from Lowestoft. It was during this period that I can most remember Lowestoft Central, as it was then called, being a bustling and very busy station. There were services to two different stations in Yarmouth (Beach and South Town), Ipswich and Norwich and connections on to London. It was during this period that I spent part of my summer holidays in the town. What I remember was the popularity of the beaches and local amenities, although in terms of shows and facilities, Lowestoft often seemed second best to nearby Yarmouth.

The decline of Lowestoft as a freight-based port began in the 1950s and it mirrored broader decline elsewhere in East Anglia. Combined with the decline in the fishing industry and the move to freightliner trains, the specific industries and needs that had been a feature of Lowestoft's goods service gradually declined in the 1960s and 1970s. However, there was still in the mid-1970s a range of freight passing through Lowestoft port to rail and today cargo is still handled at the port.

While the Beeching cuts of the late 1960s are discussed elsewhere in this volume, the locomotive shed and sleeper depot had closed a decade before. However, in 1970, when the service to Yarmouth was reduced, Lowestoft could no longer be seen as a base for holidays in the area. The replacement of steam with diesel units in 1956 resulted in a more efficient and regular service and this meant that the railway to Norwich became more of a commuter service.

Since the 1970s there have been major changes at Lowestoft station. Whilst the roof has gone, and today it looks a shadow of its former self, the station does at least offer regular and efficient trains to both Norwich and Ipswich. The lines from Norwich and Ipswich to Lowestoft survived in the 1970s and 1980s in part due to local pressure. Pressure groups of local passengers successfully lobbied for more trains and the continued popularity of special trains to London for football cup finals or works outings showed the value of the railways.

Lowestoft Railway Today

Since the 1980s there has been a revival in many local passenger services as more and more people to commute to work. Also, rail has again become a popular mode of travel particularly for younger people and the retired with concessionary fares. This can be seen in the services into and out of Lowestoft today.[6]

There are hourly services to Norwich and Ipswich with more at peak times. Various attempts to have a direct through service to London have not been sustained. The railway station, after being called a blot on the landscape by the local MP in 2010, has today been revived with new and improved parking facilities. A freight terminal remains although at much reduced capacity, with the emphasis on servicing the local offshore oil and gas industry.

Lowestoft is a classic example of a town that, to a large extent, grew as a result of having a railway which linked to elsewhere in East Anglia and beyond—London, the Midlands and the North. At its height, before and after the Second World War, the town was a bustling place, full of activity be it from fishing or local ancillary industries or holiday-makers. To me it was and remains a place with fond memories of enjoyable summer holidays, lovely beaches and enjoying local fish specialties. Although the town has been in decline since the 1960s,

Lowestoft station in 2020.

it remains a popular place for day trippers and has benefited from North Sea related industries such as oil, gas and wind turbines.

Notes

1 *White (2002) p.5.*

2 *Quoted in Cox (2008) p.54.*

3 *Brooks (1997) 'The Effects on Lowestoft of the Coming of the Railway' in Garrod (1997) pp.23-31.*

4 *Suffolk Federation of Women's Institutes (1994).*

5 *Hewison (1981).*

6 *https://www.lowestoftjournal.co.uk/news/more-passengers-on-east-suffolk-line-1-6036568*

London to Norwich

The main arterial line through East Anglia has always been that from London Liverpool Street to Norwich. It was the line the early pioneers of the railways saw as their ultimate goal. Norwich is the regional capital of East Anglia and London is the nation's capital so a regular and good service linking them was seen as critical to the success of the railways in East Anglia. The line, when it was finally developed, not only joined up these two centres but included key towns and cities, such as Ipswich, Colchester and Chelmsford.

This chapter outlines the ways in which the line evolved, the changes in timetables, rolling stock, specific incidents and what it was like to be a driver on this line. Other chapters in this volume discuss themes that had a direct impact on the success of this line, such as the Boat trains, Norwich Thorpe and Manningtree stations.

Overview of the Line

The East Anglia main line is 114½ miles long from London Liverpool Street to Norwich, via Chelmsford, Colchester and Stowmarket. Its development was by no means straightforward and its slow development was in part due to the competition of two companies, the Eastern Counties (ECR) and Eastern Union (EUR). The building of the line was also handicapped by various steep gradients along the way and having to cross low lying and marshy terrain especially around Colchester and Manningtree. Its great engineering feat was the construction of Stoke Tunnel, just south of Ipswich station.

The section of line between Colchester and Ipswich was built by the EUR to standard gauge and opened to passenger traffic in June 1846. An extension from a new junction at Haughley to Norwich Victoria opened in December 1849.

London Terminus

A major issue in those early years was securing a suitable terminus in the capital. In 1839, when the line opened to Romford, a temporary station was constructed in Mile End and called Devonshire Street. Within a few years a more permanent terminus was constructed nearer to central London in Shoreditch. The building, of Italianate design, was impressive but was located in an area well known for crime. A letter in the *Norfolk Chronicle* of July 1852 observed the 'light fingered gentry who have of late been infesting the Shoreditch Railway

Station'.[1] As soon as it became clear that the railway was going to be successful for the distribution of agricultural produce, a depot was opened in Brick Lane, near Bishopsgate, for this purpose.

By 1857 it was becoming apparent that the terminus at Shoreditch was too small and plans were drawn up for a much larger station nearby. The new station was to be called Liverpool Street but, due to financial problems within the railway company, it was not to open until 1875. The GER company, which was responsible for running the station and the line out of London, soon found that even this station would not be big enough and a more grandiose one was completed in 1894. Liverpool Street, at the time of its completion, was the busiest terminus in London. In 1903 there were 416 daily arrivals at the station. By 1912, around 200,000 passengers used the station daily on around 1,000 separate trains.

The station has been affected by wars and conflicts. The station was struck by air raids in 1917 that killed 162 people and injured over 400. On the eve of the Second World War, Liverpool Street became the final destination of thousands of Jewish refugees from continental Europe as part of the Kindertransport.

During the Second World War, the station's structure sustained damage from a nearby bomb, particularly the Gothic tower at the main entrance on Liverpool Street and its glass roof. E.J. Rudsdale remarks, upon arrival into Liverpool Street from Colchester, the impact of bomb damage on the station in June 1941:

> At Liverpool Street, the familiar dirt and noise and smell but daylight comes through the roof in unexpected places, and the great station clock is now on the ground, although still working. The station offices at Liverpool Street were burnt out and there are a few buildings burnt near Broad Street station.[2]

The station was damaged by the bombing at Bishopgate in 1993 and in 2005, seven passengers were killed when a bomb exploded aboard an underground train just after it had departed from Liverpool Street.

By the 1970s there was an urgent need to modernise the station and it was planned to finance this through property development on the site. In 1975 British Railways announced plans to demolish and redevelop it with nearby Broad Street. The proposed demolition met considerable public opposition which led to a public inquiry. The outcomes of the inquiry led to the retention of the western train shed and repairs to the main roof. The existing eighteen platform layout was retained. It did mean the final closure and demolition of Broad Street and its re-development as a new office and shopping complex, Broadgate. The re-developed Liverpool Street was officially opened by the

Liverpool Street Station, 2019.

Queen on 5 December 1991.

Liverpool Street remains the gateway to East Anglia serving commuters from Essex and day trippers from Suffolk and Norfolk. It is one of the busiest railway stations in the United Kingdom.

The First Inter-City Trains

When a direct line from London to Norwich was first proposed, there was a debate as to which was the best and quickest route. One suggestion was via Cambridge and Brandon and the other via Colchester and Ipswich. In 1843 the route from Shoreditch to Colchester was opened but it was notoriously slow, with some trains taking over two hours. It was also unpunctual and dirty. The slow development of a line out of London to Colchester and beyond meant it was the line through Cambridge that offered the first route for passengers. But by the 1860s rail travel from London to Norwich via Ipswich was faster; three and half hours compared with four via Cambridge. For the next decade or so there was concerted competition between the lines, and for a time, speed dominated with each trying to better the other. For example, in 1874 both services operated four through trains per day taking very similar times, around 290 minutes. However, by 1883, the Ipswich route was 30 minutes faster, at 207 minutes. This difference remained well into the 20th century and by 1939 there were more direct services to London via Ipswich (eight compared with six) than through Cambridge. By the 1970s this difference was even more pronounced with only one or two trains per day via Cambridge taking between three and three and half hours compared with eighteen trains via Ipswich at around two to two and a half hours.

During the 20th century, the rolling stock of the trains continued to improve. The inter-war period saw both the quality, frequency and speeds of the inter-city services increase. Timings to Colchester from London came down to 66 minutes. After 1945, following the introduction of the Britannia class, times to Colchester from London were reduced to just under an hour. Following the inauguration of diesel and electric trains in the 1960s and 1970s, travel time was gradually reduced to 45 minutes where it has remained to this day.

The line from London to Norwich was always seen as the 'flagship' line in the East Anglia and the various attempts, during the 20th century, to reduce travel time to the capital reflected this. Although considerable resources had been put into improving the quality of the rolling stock on the trains in the first decade of the century, it was only in the 1950s that one could see major attempts to improve the timetable itself. This was, in part, due to the influence of Gerard Fiennes who became Operating Superintendent for the Eastern Region in 1956.[3] His introduction of non-stop trains from London to Ipswich, and departures on the half hour, meant reaching Norwich in two hours and ten minutes.

Stratford Works

For many workers on the Eastern Region, a key centre for ensuring all the trains were fit for service was Stratford Works, just east of London. It was where many workers, drivers, firemen, maintenance men and administrative staff were based for the region as a whole. The Works became the nucleus for the construction and maintenance of locomotives in the late 19th century. When it first opened in 1848 it employed over a thousand people and this increased to over six thousand by 1912. By 1921 it was repairing over 500 freight wagons a week as well as locomotives.

It is therefore appropriate to note the observations of various workmen who were based at Stratford. These give an indication of what life was like there but also highlight some of the issues they faced on a daily basis.

In the late 19th century, as the railways became a complex business, there was not only a need for maintenance depots but also, accommodation for some men, to rest between long journeys. Both the ECR and, later, the GER, recognised the need and built a hostel at Stratford. Although lodgings were welcomed by the workers, their location, such as the one at Stratford, did not necessarily mean you got much sleep with the noise of engines moving around twenty-four hours a day. The sleeping accommodation was in a 'dormitory without windows, the ventilation coming through louvres in the roof, and it was common to wake up in the morning to find a thin layer of soot on the bed.'[4]

Stratford railway dormitory.

There are a number of memoirs by railway workers who were based at Stratford. For example, J.W. Barnes began as a cleaner at Stratford in September 1899. He progressed to be a fireman during the First World War and was made a driver in 1919. He became well known as one of the drivers for the royal trains which went up to Wolverton station for Sandringham. He was also employed as an Acting Inspector and maintained a record of each day's work, including the number of locomotives worked on.[5]

A contemporary of his was Charlie Francis who joined the Great Eastern as a cleaner in 1898. He was part of a gang who worked, at first, on tank type engines before progressing to passenger engines. Each gang had to clean five engines per shift. In 1902, like many railwaymen, he became a spare firemen, working mainly goods traffic between the yards at Stratford and Peterborough. During the First World War, he spent a lot of his time working on ambulance trains. In 1919 he was promoted to driver and his routes varied—to Norwich, Clacton and Bury St. Edmunds, as well as the goods routes to March and Peterborough. He later recalled working on the 2.50 paper train, 'down to Norwich with her and back to Liverpool Street with the 8.22'.[6] With only three hours rest, he said, he was then required to work the East London down to Croydon.

Tony Edsor joined Stratford works in 1948 with a childhood enthusiasm for railways. He was first allocated to the brass fitting shop.[7] The brass shop consisted of about five different departments dealing with brass equipment for the engines. After two years in the brass shop, he transferred to working on the lathes, turning plugs for boilers. He then transferred to the fitting shop, where he was involving in repairing sandboxes. He left the Works in 1954 to do his national service, but came back in 1956, to find he now needed to start repairing diesel engines as well as steam locomotives.

More recently we have William Robinson, who worked at Stratford in the post-war period. He described Stratford in the 1970s 'as a rambling depot, one of the biggest sheds in Europe with more loco and manpower than any other regional shed'.[8] He states there was a strong pride in working there remarking,

A typical scene at Stratford between the wars showing a goods and an empty stock train.

'most of the staff thought they were special'. He, like others, noted how complex Stratford was as a Works with several different yards—Temple Mills being the main one. Robinson's work at Stratford was mainly to do with responding to breakdowns and derailments. In 1977 he said he dealt with 287 maintenance calls.

Roger Taylor[9] arrived at Stratford in 1970. Like many who wished to be a driver, the ladder to promotion was still traditional—cleaner, fireman then eventually driver, although now the post of fireman had been replaced by that of Driver's Assistant. He reveals that, upon arriving for work at the depot, there was a hive of activity with different running sheds for various tasks—diesel units, short-term and long-term maintenance. As Roger had previously worked on the railways in Australia, he quickly became a Drivers' Assistant and learnt about signalling, how the engines worked and warning systems. A feature of his early training was to understand how the goods yard operated; Temple Mills was by then one of the largest in Europe. As he tells us, many of his early trips as a Driver's Assistant were very local, just moving freight around. Taylor learnt that driving shunting engines around the Temple Mills Yard at Stratford required a considerable amount of skill. He also learnt that many of the shunter drivers took great pride in keeping the locomotive in good condition. Some, he said, 'even went to the effort of polishing the copper pipework within the cab'.[10]

Around the same time, on the management side at Stratford, was Richard Morris who had various administration jobs there during the 1970s. He recalled that, although many of the workforce could be difficult to work with, they knew their job well.[11] What he did notice was that, with almost 200 men in the goods yard, it was a logistical jigsaw making sure every wagon was in the right place.

Ensuring that there were enough men around to cover all eventualities in their twelve-hour shifts was complex.[12]

These snapshots of the daily lives of railway workers, from the late 19th up to the late 20th century, show their working days were often long and hard. Whilst some had the opportunities to drive engines around East Anglia, the majority of the workforce were responsible for the maintenance of locomotives or for shunting work around the various yards. These brief summaries of railway workers' lives demonstrate that Stratford was, alongside Norwich, the most important depot in the Great Eastern and LNER eras as well as in the first few decades of British Railways.

By the 1960s, although there had been a significant decline in the workforce, it still had a major freight role including the new Freightliner work. The works closed in 1983 but it is still an important hub for railway staff, and today, acts as a depot for Eurostar trains from St.Pancras.

It is amazing to think, as one travels through Stratford on the train today with the transformation of the area into the Olympic Park and Westfield shopping centre, that this was once one of the busiest railway works in the country.

Ipswich Depot

One of the main depots on the line from London to Norwich was, and remains, Ipswich. Not only is it on a key point along the line linking the nation's capital with the leading city of the region, it has always been an important junction with lines going from there to Lowestoft, Felixstowe, Bury St. Edmunds, Cambridge and Peterborough. Up until the 1950s and into the 1960s there were also lines to Framlingham and Aldeburgh. Also, up to the 1980s, there was a link line from the depot to Ipswich docks which meant Ipswich was an important freight hub.

Ipswich suffered in the early years because it had been the junction between the Eastern Counties line to the south and Eastern Union line to the North, receiving little investment from either. A temporary engine shed constructed in the 1860s remained there until the 1950s! Hawkins and Reeve, in their study of engine sheds, have noted that, despite poor working conditions, 'a long and illustrious tradition of high quality craftsmanship' developed.[13] With over a hundred locomotives based there prior to the outbreak of the First World War, its importance cannot be underestimated. Hawkins and Reeve also report that into the early decades of the 20th century, it employed more men than Norwich. Even in the 1920s, there were over 80 men employed on locomotive repairs with over 100 on the footplate.[14] The state of the engine sheds remained an issue well into the 1960s. There was minimal space in which to work and everyday facilities were clearly insufficient. There were very primitive toilets and there was nowhere to wash or eat. In the 1920s repair work was being transferred from Ipswich to Stratford. Further re-organisation began in the 1950s with the rebuilding of the shed and the introduction of diesels towards the end of the decade.

The new depot, the first in the country to be converted entirely from steam to diesel, had 27 diesel engines and over twenty diesel shunters in the early 1960s.

Ipswich, despite its shortcomings, was regarded by the its workforce as a good place to be. There were always opportunities for a range of jobs and promotion. In the late 1940s and early 1950s, for example, more than 90 locomotives were based there. There was a lot of shed-based shunting work as well as opportunities for firemen and drivers on local branch lines, as well as the main line. Richard Hardy, who took over as Ipswich shedmaster in 1950, was responsible for over 50 locomotives and 450 staff that included footplatemen, cleaners, clerical and storekeepers.[15] Ipswich's reputation for high quality craftsmen preceded it, including three chargehand examining fitters who were responsible for the examination on a daily basis of all locomotives.

Hardy found it an 'extraordinary' place with very individualistic ways of working. Firemen, despite having formal uniforms, often still wore unusual clothing with cloth caps. Although he found the facilities for maintenance work inadequate and out of date, the men he said, treasured their steam engines.[16]

There are many stories of drivers based at Ipswich. Drivers, like in many depots, had a great pride in and treasured their engines. George Dennant, for example, referred to his locomotive as 'my old gal'.[17]

Ken Freestone, in 1947, following his first day of employment, stated how proud he was to be a cleaner. However, he quickly found it to be a dangerous and challenging place to work. 'The buildings and working conditions were Victorian with no sign of modernisation at all.' This, he said, resulted in great admiration for his fellow workmen who had to work under such conditions.[18]

Key Incidents and Accidents

Railway accidents occur for many reasons but a lot of them are the result of poor maintenance often combined with human error. A number of fatal accidents have occurred on the line throughout its history. An early example was in 1840 at Brentwood when four people were killed. In the early years of the line, minor accidents were a regular occurrence, as a correspondent of the *Railway Record* in 1845 recorded:

> It appears that two miles below Romford a spare engine is kept in readiness for the purpose of propelling such trains, owing to the wretched inefficiency of the plant, as may appear to be in need of assistance up the incline to Brentwood. And further it seems the driver is allowed to run his

> assistant engine on to the train while it is in motion. On Friday last the collision was sufficiently violent to floor the passengers on the whole train and snap the coupling irons... many passengers injured.[19]

There was another fatality in 1872 at Kelvedon when one person was killed and sixteen injured in a derailment. But one of the worst was in 1905, at Witham, when eleven were killed and seventy-one injured as a result of derailment. The 9.27am train from Liverpool Street to Cromer was passing through Witham at high speed when all of the coaches, minus the engine and tender, left the rails just before the station. The catastrophic nature of the crash is best summarised in this report of the accident:

> Most of the vehicles of the train would appear to have left the rails a short distance before reaching the station; the engine, tender, and three leading vehicles while running through the station apparently broke loose from the rest of the train, and ran on alone; these vehicles also parted company from each other at the down end of the station, and they all came to rest at different points a short distance beyond the platform. No case of fatal injury occurred in these vehicles. The next five vehicles, some of which fouled the down island platform, were badly derailed, and suffered very severe damage; the fifth and sixth vehicles were both found lying on the down platform; the former was thrown over on to its side, and it crashed into the porters' and ticket collectors' rooms, completely wrecking them and killing a porter who was in them at the time the latter vehicle was completely overturned and the top framework of it was entirely smashed to atoms by the weight of the wheels and underframe. Eight passengers, who were riding in this last vehicle, were killed instantaneously, and a child who was also riding in it succumbed later to his injuries. One other passenger in the train was killed by the accident, but it was not definitely known in which carriage he was riding. ... In addition to the ten passengers and one porter who were killed, sixty-six passengers and five railway employees were injured.[20]

A hero that day was the driver, Fred Hubbard, who managed to stop the up train from Cromer before it encountered the wreckage of the down *Cromer Express* at Witham.[21]

This remains to this day the worst single loss of life in a railway accident in Essex.

At first it was assumed that the accident was the result of the speed of the train but later evidence showed that a 'key was out of the rail' where three platelayers had been working and they had failed to check the rail.

In the second decade of the 20th century there were a number of incidents. At Colchester, in 1913, three were killed and fourteen injured in a collision and derailment. The inquiry into this incident concluded it was primarily due to signalman error when the *Norfolk Coast Express* ran into the back of an engine. The driver, fireman and guard of the Express train were killed. The signalman, while he admitted his error, was dismissed by the Great Eastern Railway and concerns were raised by his trade union and the local press that to whether he had been treated too harshly.[22]

However, it was in 1915, at Ilford, that a major tragedy occurred when ten people were killed and five hundred injured as a result of a collision between two trains. On 1 January 1915, the driver and the firemen of an express from Clacton to London Liverpool Street failed to see signals at danger. Despite the waving of a red flag by a signalman, the train continued on its journey and hit a local service from Gidea Park to Liverpool Street that was passing over from the branch to the main line. The official report attributed blame to the driver of the Clacton train for his 'insufficient care in noting the positions of his signals when approaching Ilford'. But if one looks more closely at the report weather conditions were poor. There was thick fog and, despite detonators being used to attract attention, they were not heard. The report recommended that automatic warning systems were urgently needed on the route.

Unfortunately, some of the lessons from this accident were not heeded and, on the same stretch of line during the Second World War, a series of accidents occurred. In 1941, seven people were killed in a collision between two trains near Brentwood. In 1944 at Ilford again, nine were killed and 38 injured. In this case the driver of an express from Yarmouth to London failed to see several signals 'at caution', but had stopped just past a signal 'at danger'. The driver walked to the nearest signal box and got the all clear to go ahead. However, as the driver returned to his train, the signalman received the warning that a following train had also passed signals 'at danger'. Aware of the emergency, the Ilford station inspector decided to place detonators at the rear of the first train. He was too late as the second train ran into the back of the first at speed of some 20-25 miles per hour. There were nine fatalities as a consequence of the collision, including Frank Heilgers, the Member of Parliament for Bury St. Edmunds. Twenty-eight people were hospitalised and ten others suffered minor injuries. Another accident, at nearby Romford in December 1944, resulted in one killed and three injured in a collision between two trains.

Pressures on Drivers and Firemen

These incidents demonstrate that it was all too easy to blame drivers for several of these accidents. The conditions under which they had to drive these steam locomotives in winter, and often in fog, not surprisingly led to accidents. Wartime conditions contributed in some cases, especially when, at night, electric signals could not be used during the Second World War.

In the 19th century being a train driver was hazardous requiring considerable skill while working non-stop under very difficult conditions. The writings of Michael Reynolds provide the clearest indication of the relationship between driver and his locomotive during this period. In *Engine Driving Life: Stirring Adventures and Incidents in the Lives of Locomotive Engine-Drivers*, Reynolds depicts a railway landscape beset with peril and adventure as any storm-tossed sea, requiring locomotive crews to 'exhibit heroism as genuine as that which graces a battle-field: men who die at the post of duty, in all the pride of manhood, turned by erring hands into the valley of the shadow of death.'[23]

Driving a Train on the Line in the 1970s and 1980s.

Nearly a century later, Roger Taylor's memories of driving trains on the London to Norwich line shows that, although the life of a driver was physically less arduous, mentally, it was probably even more pressured with long hours and constantly changing work patterns.

At first, he was still a Driver's Assistant explaining the long and unsocial hours they had to work.

> We worked the 19.30 departure from Liverpool Street to Norwich and then returned with the 23.15 mail train via Cambridge and didn't get back to Stratford until after two in the morning.[24]

He noted that you could be away from home for a long time and had few opportunities to engage in a social life. Despite this, railwaymen, particularly drivers, had their own sense of humour. A typical passenger's request might be 'how long to the next train'. The reply that came back was 'about four coaches, mate'.[25] Another was 'Are you going to Cambridge?" The reply being 'No', followed by a short pause and then 'But that train that we are not hooked up to is'.[26]

In 1976 he applied to be a driver but failed the exam as he could not remember key facts from the Rule Book. A few months later, at his second attempt, he passed and began full driver training in February 1977. Developing the skills to be an effective train driver took time and a lot of his early work was on shunting and freight work. As he began to take on more responsibility, he found himself in the middle of the controversial change to abolish Assistant Drivers. Single manned working was already in operation at the time on local suburban lines, and some of the tasks for the Assistant, such as headcodes for engines and signal look out, no longer became necessary with colour light signals and cabs having good all-round visibility.

Taylor developed his skills as a driver first being an assistant and learning on the job. One particular skill was to bring the train to a full stop at the appropriate place on the platform in a smooth way. He recalls how he developed this to perfection while arriving at Colchester station on route to London by knowing when and how to apply 'full service' and in relation to the gradient slowing down the engine. 'The art came', he said, 'in having the confidence in the equipment that one was using'.[27]

From Diesel Haul to Electrification

As discussed in a later chapter, the Britannia steam locomotives were the iconic face of the line in the 1950s. They provided fast and efficient trains but they were the last steam-hauled trains on the main line from Norwich to London and, in the late 1950s, were gradually replaced by diesel-electric locomotives. Their introduction resulted in a major reorganisation of the timetable.

It was electrification, however, that was seen as the long-term solution for the whole line. As it gradually became electrified, first to Colchester, then to Ipswich, and eventually Norwich by the 1980s, newer and faster locomotives were introduced. This also meant more trains. The opening of a new depot for these locomotives at Norwich Crown Point in 1982 also ensured a much smoother and more efficient approach to maintenance and readiness for service for the trains.

Now, in the third decade of the 21st century, comes the latest major change—the introduction of twelve carriages in 2020 with the new Aventra trains.[28] Like many inter-city lines, the London to Norwich line became increasingly popular in the first two decades of the 21st century. Use has more than doubled at many of the stations, with the most significant increases being those the greatest distance from London. For 2017/18, the passenger entries and exits for the three main stations were as follows:

- Colchester: 4,378,758
- Norwich: 4,156,302
- Ipswich: 3,351,902.[29]

As trains became faster and more frequent, people began to commute to London from further away. Today, it is places beyond Colchester, such as Manningtree, Ipswich and Diss, that have seen the biggest increases in passenger use.

The London to Norwich mainline remains the 'flagship' route for the Great

Ipswich station with new rolling stock.

Eastern. It has always been the line where the new locomotives and carriages are first introduced. It has also always been the most popular line in terms of passenger numbers in East Anglia.

Notes

1 *Gale (2015) p.101.*

2 *Pearson (2010).*

3 *Fiennes (1973).*

4 *Quoted in McKenna (1980).*

5 *Portrait. Top link drivers, No. 107. Railway Magazine, 1949, 95, 309.*

6 *Ibid. p.42.*

7 *Edsor, An Apprentice, M & GN Oral Histories no.6.*

8 *Robinson (2005) p.127.*

9 *Taylor (2008).*

10 *Ibid. p.82.*

11 *Morris (2012).*

12 *Ibid.*

13 *Hawkins and Reeve (1987) p.221.*

14 *Ibid.*

15 *Richard Hardy Remembers, M & GN Society Oral Histories no.2.*

16 *Ibid.*

17 *Ibid.*

18 *Freestone and Smith, p.182.*

19 *quoted in Gordon, p.30.*

20 *Board of Trade Accident Report in http://www.railwaysarchive.co.uk/docsummary.php?docID=2496*

21 *Locomotive Magazine 1917, 23, 62.*

22 *An excellent account of this tragic accident can be found in Connor (2003).*

23 *http://www.steamindex.com/people/drivers.htm*

24 *Taylor p.67.*

25 *Ibid. p.68.*

26 *Ibid.*

27 *Ibid. p.85.*

28 *https://www.edp24.co.uk/news/greater-anglia-new-trains-end-overcrowding-1-6253057*

29 *https://www.greateranglia.co.uk/about-us/news-desk/news-articles/revealed-busiest-stations-greater-anglia-network*

The Evolution of Railways at Norwich

Norwich is the premier city of East Anglia and has been the focal point as a destination and the starting point of railways in the region. For me, Norwich has always been seen as the main hub of the railway network, the place where you changed trains for going on to the Norfolk coast. For most, this has been Norwich Thorpe station, just south of the city centre, but at one time, the city boasted three stations. As well as Thorpe, there was Norwich City and Norwich Victoria. This chapter outlines the history of these three stations and the observations and experiences of different railway workers on working at and from there. The chapter will also summarise other important events which have made an impact on the stations—war, accidents, and in the cases of City and Victoria, their eventual demise.

Thorpe Station

Norwich Thorpe is the only station still in existence and remains the terminus for the line from London Liverpool Street. The first station, built to the east on land that later became the goods depot, served the Yarmouth and Norwich railway and opened in 1844. The following year this expanded to include a line to the south west of the city reaching Brandon on the Suffolk and Norfolk border. The early development of the station was hampered by the constant rivalry between two railway companies, Eastern Union (EUR) and the Eastern Counties (ECR). While the ECR used this station, the EUR, in competition, established a new station named after a pleasure garden upon which it was built, the Victoria Gardens. To distinguish them, the ECR renamed its station Norwich Thorpe.

Despite this rivalry, Thorpe station remained the dominant station. Once all the routes were amalgamated into the Great Eastern Railway in 1862, new lines were destined for the Thorpe site. These included a line to Cromer opening in 1874. Expansion necessitated a completely new station just north of the original. Opened in 1886, it is this structure which survives to this day with its impressive central clock tower.

With further amalgamations and the growth of holiday traffic to the Norfolk coastal resorts, Thorpe station continued to attract passengers. For example, in

The original 'Thorpe' station, 1845.

the 1920s, a typical weekday included thirty trains to Lowestoft and Yarmouth, six to Dereham and Lynn, about twelve to Cromer and eight or nine trains to London Liverpool Street with a similar number to Cambridge and then onto London Kings Cross. There were also stopping trains calling at Ipswich.

Although it was bombed during the Second World War, the damage to the station was much less than that at the Norwich City Station. Like most large stations that were bombed, it took a little while to re-establish all of its services from pre-war days. The emphasis was put on trains to London and, in the post-war period, some of the trains to the capital were given special names such as the *Norfolkman* and *East Anglian*.

Upon the closure of the City station, the name Thorpe was dropped and it reverted to being just Norwich.

The continued development of the station was helped by electrification of the main line to London in the 1980s, the growth of Norwich as a major regional centre and the continued popularity of services to the coastal towns of Cromer, Yarmouth and Lowestoft, as well as cross country services to Cambridge, Peterborough and beyond. Use of the station has also been helped by its proximity to Norwich City football club ground.

Norwich Victoria

The station was opened by EUR in 1849 and acted as a terminus for trains to Ipswich. The station was built on the site of a former circus and entertainment centre and some of its buildings were used within the new station.[1] Its opening was apparently a grand affair with the station decorated with flags, bunting and evergreens.[2]

Norwich Victoria railway station.

The station had two platforms arranged in an unusual V shape with a small garden between. Passenger services to the station in 1850 started at Colchester and there were three direct trains a day to Victoria. Once the GER had been created, the continued viability of the station began to be questioned. Passengers coming into Victoria station, who then wanted to go on to coastal towns, had initially to make their own way across the city. A link line to Thorpe station opened in 1851 and thereafter the station only served four or five trains each day. A 1906 timetable from the station shows this limited service but also shows that there was competition from Thorpe with some trains dividing at Tivetshall.

Although the station survived until the outbreak of war in 1914, it was closed to passenger traffic in 1916. Despite this, the station continued and developed as a major freight depot, particularly for coal and cement. Only in the 1960s was the station site finally run down, remaining a coal depot until the 1980s, when electrification and rationalisation of goods traffic made it no longer viable as a separate terminus.

Today there is no evidence of the station apart from some arches of a bridge which formed a link between the station and the main line.[3] However, in 2020, the area where the sidings had once been became the home for the fleet of new trains, with new lines and facilities.[4]

Norwich City

The third station to open in Norwich was City which opened in 1882 as part of the Lynn and Fakenham Railway. Built on the north west side of the city and just outside the city walls, it provided good access to the centre for shopping. The station later became the southern terminus of the Midland and Great Northern. Like Victoria, its creation was the result of conflicts between the various railway companies, in this case between the M & GN and the GER. Its impressive façade of red and cream brick with nine side arches and a central archway provided entrance to the platforms. There were four platforms with very ornate iron pillars and canopies. In addition, it had a substantial engine shed and turntable and extensive goods yards. At one stage, in the early 1900s, more than fifty companies used the goods facilities.

Norwich City Station.

The station was well-used, with services to Cromer and through-carriages to a range of destinations, including Peterborough and Leicester. In 1887, five years after opening, City had six or seven departures in the day with Melton Constable being the main hub to various routes across Norfolk and beyond. This level of service continued up to and beyond the First World War including a daily express to the Midlands.

Between the wars, despite the amalgamation of the M & GN into the LNER, the range of service continued with, by then, two express services per day to the Midlands. During this period there were five stopping and two fast trains from Melton Constable.

My mother used the daily service from her family home in Melton Constable to Norwich for a couple of years, at the outbreak of war, whilst she was working in the city. She found it a very good service, much quicker than going round via Cromer to Thorpe, and nearer to her place of work.

Alan Baker started working at Norwich City station aged fourteen in 1944 as a greaser, someone who oils the wheels on the locomotives, the coaches and the freight wagons. What he quickly learnt was the pride his fellow workmen took in their job and also about always wearing the appropriate clothes for a particular job:

> We wore bib and brace and a jacket [but my foreman, Bert] did not want me to get my working clothes dirty.[5]

The station was badly bombed during the Norwich blitz of April 1942. The engine shed was damaged beyond repair and most of the ornate pillars and façade were also badly damaged. The station was further damaged, along with St Philips Church, when in November 1944, a badly damaged USAF B24 Liberator bomber, the Lady Jane, was deliberately crashed there to avoid civilian casualties.

Although the City station survived and services were soon up and running, it became a drab concrete building with no impressive arches and was open to the elements with only one platform roof.

The hazards of working as a cleaner during this period can be seen in this memory from Alan Baker. Although it was just after the war, 1946, there were still periodic blackouts due to shortages. He later recalled:

> I was on the back of the tender cleaning the tank filler lid from quite a considerable amount of coal. While we were busy doing that, the lights went out and we were left in the dark. I thought I was well on the tank, but no, I was on the edge and as I stepped back for another shovelful, I fell over the back of the tender and hit the buffer with my side. I sustained severe internal injuries.[6]

Baker commented that he was very lucky to be alive, having had a kidney and part of his liver removed, and that, when he had a medical aged, 60, the doctor said he should never have become a driver.

My only memories of City station are from as a young child in the 1950s. It was still then a busy station with nine weekday trains to Melton Constable with two of them carrying carriages on to the Midlands. By 1958, diesel multiple units had replaced steam with nine up and down trains on weekdays and two more on Saturdays. Passenger numbers in this year, although significantly in decline compared with pre-war numbers, still showed the value of the station. In June of that year, on average, 324 people arrived and 350 departed each working day, with 588 and 552 at weekends. Despite this, the following year, the station closed to passenger services along with much of the M & GN. It did remain a goods and freight depot until 1969.

Commemorative sculpture to Norwich City station.

Unlike Victoria station, one can still see some of the platforms, the site of the turntable and engine sheds. The site of the station has also been remembered by the erection of a sculpture, plaques and crossing gates. A local group, Friends of Norwich City Station (FONCS), has been preserving the buildings that survive and they plan to develop a memorial garden.

Norwich Shed and Railwaymen

Working at Norwich, which usually meant being based at Thorpe station, was often seen by many railwaymen as the pinnacle of their career although once you were there, there were few opportunities for further career progression. It was, and remains, the main railway hub for the region. Even as late as 1958, there were about 400 enginemen at Norwich with about a hundred mechanical and workshop staff. From its early days up to the 1980s, when Crown Point was opened, the main workplace for Norwich railwaymen was in the sheds by the side of Thorpe station. These provided a 'home' for the engines where regular maintenance and the occasional overhaul took place.

George Ewles was a typical railwayman based at Thorpe during the early decades of the 20th century. After watching trains as a boy in rural Norfolk, he began at Thorpe as a cleaner in 1919. He then went to Stratford, where he became a fireman returning to Norwich, in 1925. He later became a driver staying there until his retirement in 1966. During the 1950s he was one of the main drivers for the Britannia class, the engine *Oliver Cromwell* his main locomotive. In the early 1960s he drove diesel electric locomotives and for the last few years up, to his retirement, he was responsible for diesel multiple units. Ewles was typical of many drivers based at Norwich in stating how proud he was to be driving a locomotive.[7]

Bill Harvey, in his memories of working there from 1947 to 1970, suggests that, whilst it was a busy place to work, it 'was an ambling old place with many holes and corners'. He was responsible for the maintenance of steam locomotives which, when he started working there, numbered 120. Among the many challenges he faced was ensuring the locomotives had a constant supply of water. This was a problem at certain times of the year because the water came from tidal reservoirs. The introduction of diesels and the relocation of the main depot to Crown Point resolved this issue.[8]

At Thorpe, Harvey saw first hand the impact of nationalisation in 1948 and the change in working patterns that resulted. Changes came in locomotive maintenance, an increased recognition of the working conditions of railwaymen and that staff needed to be kept better informed of new equipment and the priorities of the railway. 1958 saw important adjustments at Norwich, with new management systems, the transfer to Norwich of mechanical maintenance to all Britannia class locomotives and the introduction of diesel-electric locomotives. With 87 steam locomotives based in the city, alongside a fleet of 47 railcars, nearly 800 men were still employed at the depot. However, in the following years, Harvey had to deal with the move of drivers to diesel powered trains and more locomotives with no extra staff.

British Railways (BR) had agreed to continue to employ workers who found they could no longer do the job they had originally trained for. For example, it honoured its obligation to employ 6% of war disabled men. It meant, according to Harvey, that you often ended up with the wrong type of workers in particular posts. However, he did note the valuable experience of ex-drivers, some of whom were classed as disabled on account of being colour blind. Harvey found they took great pride and interest in their new duties.[9]

Harvey felt, for the first few years of his time in Norwich, he did not have the authority required for his assigned role. This was, in part, due to the continuation of pre-war staffing roles. The introduction of rest days for footplate workers and the reduction in working hours were added complications. Although new staff were recruited, he was involved in their appointment and he often found that they were not suited to railway work. Only with re-organisation of the station, in 1958, did he feel he fully became a shedmaster.

Harvey reflects many of the challenges railway workmen faced in the 1940s and 1950s dealing with poor management structures and pre-nationalisation working practices. It was only in the late 1950s and early 1960s that changes introduced saw any benefits.

The Thorpe Railway Disaster 1874[10]

Railways were often prone to accidents with frequent fatalities. It was at Norwich that one of the most horrific of these accidents took place on 10 September 1874. At the time it was considered to be the worst railway accident in Britain when, on a wet evening, two trains ended up on the same track at Thorpe St. Andrew just outside the city. The resulting collision resulted in 27 deaths.

One of the trains was the Yarmouth mail train carrying passengers, freight and post. It had thirteen carriages and had an experienced driver in John Prior.

Coming into Norwich, the line changed from double track at Brundall to a single track into the city. At Brundall, the mail train would usually wait on a loop for the line to become clear before finishing the last stretch of its journey. At Thorpe station the expected 9.17pm express train from London was late, which was quite a normal occurrence at this time. The express arrived at 9.23 and with a seven minute turnaround, left the station at 9.30. In those fateful seven minutes, a message had been sent via telegraph to inform the mail train that it could proceed into Thorpe. Once it was realised that an error had been made, another telegram was sent calling for the mail train to be halted. But it was too late, neither trains could be stopped.

The dramatic illustration of the disaster on the cover of the Illustrated London News, 19 September 1874.

The driver of the express, Thomas Clarke, was keen to make up his lost time and the trains collided at a combined speed of around 60 mph just beyond the eastern rail bridge. The Norwich train engine ended up on top of the mail train and drivers and firemen of both trains were instantly killed. There were 25 fatalities among the passengers and 73 seriously injured.[11]

The track itself was only slightly damaged and the line was back in operation by mid-afternoon the following day.[12] Ironically, two tracks had recently been installed on the section of the line where the accident occurred and the work was awaiting approval following an inspection.[13]

The accident led to considerable discussion in the newspapers as to railway safety and improvements were made to ensure such an event did not occur again. The introduction of the tablet[14] for use on single track lines was a consequence of this, and other similar accidents, around this time.

This accident showed that, even fifty years after the establishment of the passenger railway service in the UK, it could still be a hazardous form of travel. However, the legacy of the Thorpe disaster, alongside others during this period, did have an impact on encouraging a more safety conscious industry.

Notes

1 *http://www.disused-stations.org.uk/n/norwich_victoria/index.shtml*

2 *https://www.edp24.co.uk/home/take-a-look-back-at-norwich-s-forgotten-railway-station-1-4704072*

3 *http://www.disused-stations.org.uk/n/norwich_victoria/index.shtml*

4 *https://www.greateranglia.co.uk/about-us/news-desk/news-articles/norwich-victoria-sidings-now-in-use-biggest-infrastructure-project*

5 *Baker (2019) p.8.*

6 *Ibid. p.14.*

7 *Brodribb (1994).*

8 *Harvey (1986).*

9 *Ibid.*

10 *http://www.broadlandmemories.co.uk/blog/author/broadlandmemories/*

11 *https://www.gersociety.org.uk/index.php/files-emporium-home/rh029-the-official-report-into-the-fatal-collision-near-norwich-in-1874?search=accident*

12 *http://www.broadlandmemories.co.uk/blog/2014/09/the-thorpe-railway-disaster-1874/)*

13 *https://www.greatyarmouthmercury.co.uk/your-great-yarmouth/nostalgia/the-filthy-night-when-two-trains-collided-1-3737110*

14 *The tablet was a large token the driver was given by a signalman when they entered single track line. Only when they gave up the tablet at the place where the line reverted to double track could another train pass through the single track line.*

Melton Constable: The Crewe Of East Anglia

Melton Constable, a village in mid-Norfolk has a very special place in my memories of the railways in East Anglia. It is also key to my own family history. My mother's father, George Kinsley, worked at Melton Constable from the early 1920s to the early 1960s. He was a wheeltapper and his job was to inspect every carriage and engine on its arrival at the station. My father moved to the village in 1940 to work in the locomotive sheds as a young cleaner and it was there he met my mother and they were married in Melton in 1942. Melton Constable was a place I got to know very well as a child. The family went on holiday there for a week every year, using the railway station to go to the beaches at Sheringham and Cromer and explore the Norfolk countryside. My grandparents were active members of the local community, involved with the local bowls team and visitors to the Railway Institute, the social club for railway workers.

Therefore, I have a very strong affection for the village. Melton Constable was rather untypical of Norfolk villages, being more like a Northern mining community with its line of terraced houses and linked social activities. Above all, as this chapter will demonstrate, Melton Constable typified the strong bond workmen had with the railway, for them it was more than a job, it was part of who they were.

The author's grandfather, George Kinsley.

Formation of the Station

Before the advent of railways, Melton Constable was a tiny

village of nineteen houses and 100 people employed by Lord Hastings on his estate. It was not an ideal place to develop a railway junction with no nearby labour supply, poor soil conditions and a marked slope through the proposed gap in which the station would be built.

The site was chosen because Lord Hastings, the local landowner, offered the land in return for shares on the line. He was a Director of the Lynn & Fakenham line and set aside land to the northeast of his Melton estate for the establishment of the station and a new junction. In supporting the development of the railway, Lord Hastings insisted on having his own platform and waiting room with its own private entrance. There was also a belief that there was once an underground passage running under the track to the Refreshment room opposite so the staff could easily provide his Lordship's guests with refreshments when required.

With no habitation of any size in the village, effectively a new community had to be established. Initially 28 houses were built but these were soon seen as insufficient. In 1886 another area of houses was built although this time were regarded as being of poorer quality.

The work on the railway station and adjacent works began in 1881. The line opened in 1882 through to Norwich and the line from North Walsham and Yarmouth, which joined the Norwich line at Melton East Junction, opened in April 1883. Meanwhile a start was made on a line to the west, first to Holt and then eastwards to Cromer in 1887. During the same period another line going west to Lynn was also opened.

Passengers waiting at Melton Constable station, c1957.

The station at Melton Constable was of an unusual design with a long island platform with space for more than one train on the platform at any time. A goods yard was also developed, which initially had three lines, later becoming six, that served a large goods shed, three cattle pens and coal yard. Alongside the creation of the station, and in response to the need for a headquarters for repairs and offices for engineers, a Locomotive and Carriage Works was founded in 1881. It included an Engineers office, foundry, erecting shop, carriage shop, machine shop and smithy.

At its height, in the early decades of the 20th century, Melton station included island platforms for passengers, extensive sidings, turntable, engine

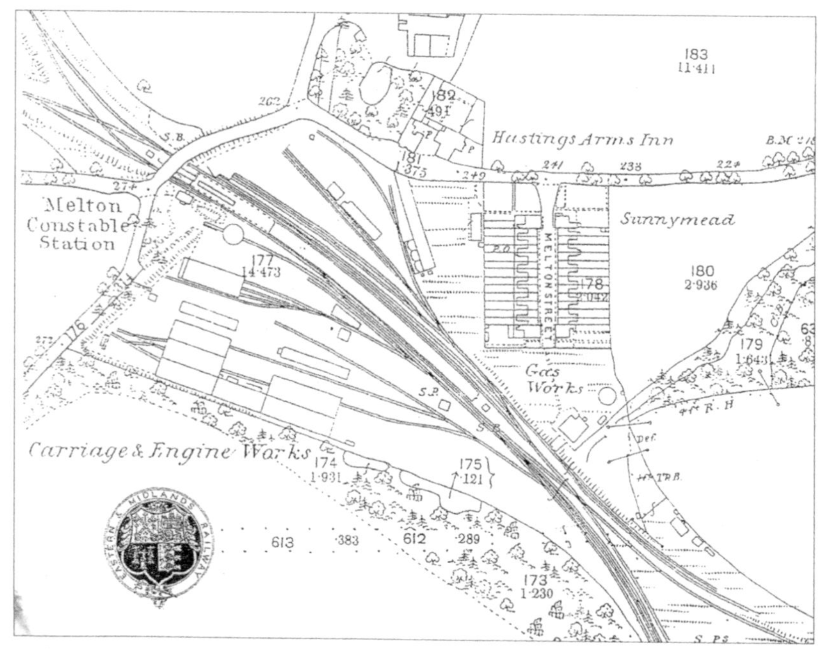

Melton Constable station layout.

shed, foundry, offices and stores, messroom, fitting shop, paint shop, carriage and wagon shop, tender shop and boiler shop. There was always activity and constant development.

A Railway Village for All

At the turn of the 20th century, Melton resembled a mining village with its streets of terrace houses and, at beginning and end of the day, lines of workmen walking to and from their place of work in the various fitting and repair sheds. This industrial flavour could also be heard from the 'buzzer' summoning men to work. Melton Street, the first of the streets to have these terraced houses was built in 1882 by the railway company for its workers. All houses were supplied with gas from the railway gas works and running water.

Melton's turntable in action in the 1950s.

The employees' rent and water charges were deducted from their wages, along with 4d a week for membership of the Institute, the local social club. When they left the Company's employ or retired, they had to vacate their houses.

Melton developed two types of housing. On the west side of the main street, and off it, were railway houses. On the other side and adjacent roads were private houses. These private houses were larger with bay windows. The population in 1881 was 188 and had trebled in size within a decade. By 1911 the village had grown to 1,157 residents.

As a village, Melton became in the years up to and immediately after the First World War, a thriving community with many local amenities, several shops including Co-op, butchers, chemist, drapers, hairdressers, post offices.

Lord Hastings and his family continued to have an influence on the development of Melton. They paid for the elementary school which was built in 1896. But his son, on taking over the estate, refused to support further expansion of the station because it would have meant demolishing their private waiting room.

Up to 1914, the station site was in constant development and constant activity. Workers up to the outbreak of World War I had no paid holiday. The works simply closed for a full week in August. During the war, the machine shops also helped make war armaments, including shells, with more than 30,000 being produced.

A Busy Railway Junction

Traffic through Melton Constable was heavy with trains approaching from four directions. Melton was often the place where trains were divided up or combined into longer trains. This combining of trains into one, particularly for going west to the Midlands, continued into the inter-war period and then again up to the 1950s.

In 1882 there were six through trains on a weekday from Kings Lynn through Melton to Norwich or Yarmouth. By 1891 this had increased to eight between Lynn and Melton although the number through to Norwich remained six.

Locomotives at Melton Constable, c1957.

By the summer of 1938 there were six trains from South Lynn to Melton, one of these being an express through to Yarmouth. Even as late as 1958/9, the timetable showed six services between South

Lynn and Melton. These connected with trains to Norwich City station.

Although there were many trains passing through the station every day, it was not a busy station in terms of passengers either starting or ending their journeys there. It was a small community and the surrounding hinterland was rural. Its importance was more as a junction, a point midway between South Lynn and Yarmouth. Trains passed on their way to places as far afield as Birmingham and Leicester, and I can remember in the 1950s still being excited by seeing an express pass through from the Midlands on the way to the coast with holiday makers.

Although the station and the works became less important after 1945, and into the following decade, it was still a busy place. For example, in the early 1950s, there was an arrival or departure ever 30 minutes or so. The majority of departures were two trains to South Lynn, Norwich and Cromer respectively.

A list of some of the departures in 1952 gives a flavour of the level of activity and the distance and range of destinations:

6.36	Norwich
7.05	Liverpool Street
7.17	Yarmouth
7.30	Peterborough
7.49	Norwich
8.36	Peterborough
9.34	Yarmouth
9.37	Norwich
10.28	Birmingham
11.45	Peterborough
11.50	Liverpool Street
13.30	Yarmouth
13.32	Norwich
14.20	Peterborough
14.25	Cromer
15.10	Peterborough

Passengers always had the problem regarding the best route to London—west on the M & GN to Peterborough and down to Kings Cross, or east, via Cromer and Norwich to Liverpool Street. The latter, run by the rival Great Eastern, was much quicker. This meant that by offering both directions, Melton did not effectively service either. Where it was more efficient was in linking the

Midlands with the east coast. By 1900 you could get from Leicester to Melton in 2 hours 45 minutes with another 45 minutes to Norwich.

The summer season was always a busy time for Melton even up to the late 1950s. For example, on Saturday 1 August 1958, a hundred trains were scheduled to pass through or terminate at the station. This of course meant a very hectic period for the railwaymen at the station. This does not tell all of the story at such times. A considerable number of these trains split or were joined at the station meaning increased work for drivers, guards and signalmen. In addition, there was also the continuous goods and shunting work that went on at such a busy junction.

It was a station where people either stretched their legs, whilst the train was either coupled or de-coupled, or where you changed trains. This meant the refreshment room was very busy at all hours of the day and night. Reginald Gamble spoke about when his mother was manager in the early 1900s and said how busy it was particularly when the special trains from Kings Cross to Yarmouth required changing engines or coaches at the station.[1]

The station was so busy during the first half of the 20th century a W.H. Smith bookstall on the platform, one of the few on the M & GN network, was thought viable and profitable.

Influence of Marriott

The most important figure in the transformation of Melton was William Marriott who was a qualified engineer. He was born in Switzerland and came to England in 1868 taking Articles with Ransome's at Ipswich. In 1881, he became assistant engineer on the Lynn & Fakenham line and, two years later, became Locomotive Superintendent of the East and Midlands Railway. At the age of 26, he was possibly the youngest engineer on the railway since Stephenson and Brunel. His responsibilities grew upon the merger that created the M & GN and combining engineer with traffic manager until his retirement in 1924. He died in 1943 at Sheringham.

Marriott was involved with the initial development of Melton. He noted in his memoirs that, during an early visit to the place, he saw the 'foundations of the shops and parts of the walls' being constructed.[2] He oversaw the development of the lines around Melton. He remarks in his memoirs that, 'we opened up in Melton Constable in 1883 and I had to work very hard to be ready'. Marriott played a major role in improving the quality of the line's track. Conscious of the need to set an example and to understand the views of the workforce, he decided in 1885 to move to Melton. His memoirs state:

I felt if success was to be assured I must go to live among the men. Melton

> had at that time a very bad reputation. A new staff had been collected from all sorts of places and contained a certain proportion of men who had been failures elsewhere. Mr. Read, the managing director, told me that if I had settled to live in such an outlandish and forsaken place, at any rate the company would not charge me any rent...[3]

This sense of isolation and the challenges of getting a good workforce at Melton was Marriott's major priority. He was instrumental in ensuring the construction of new houses with proper facilities.

Marriott's success in developing Melton was in ensuring the workforce were well paid and had good houses. His reflections by the 1920s state, 'we have developed a very good staff ... with men saying, "we have gentleman's lives compared to what we use to have"'.[4]

During the First World War, Melton Constable's importance can be seen by the extent to which it became the home for many soldiers.

Marriott was very influential in the development of prefabricated concrete buildings on the site and the design of several locomotives, but his biggest challenge was keeping the line running on a shoestring. He remained popular and respected by workmen despite having a rather stern and traditional approach.

From M & GN to LNER and Inevitable Decline

During much of its existence the M & GN was known as *Muddle and Get Nowhere* line—but these days, people say it should be called *Missed and Greatly Needed* line. Many of the men employed as navvies were ex-farm labourers attracted by the 50% increase over their normal agricultural wages.

The M & GN developed a reputation as a smartly run operation. The staff at Melton, for example, wore dark green corduroy uniforms. Engineering staff particularly were known to be well trained.

Although Melton and the M & GN came under London and North Eastern Railway (LNER) in 1936, it still retained, up to nationalisation, a distinctive identity. However, this strong pride in the company hid underlying problems in terms of efficiency and effectiveness. The poor state of the track was, for example, given as the main reason for the accident at Hindolveston in 1937, just outside Melton, when a three-coach passenger train got derailed on a curve. What became clear was that the pebble base of the track had been badly maintained. The engineering works closed in 1936 and this had a major impact upon the village.

The Second World War provided temporary relief with the need for stores and repair workshops. It was during the war that my father first came to work at Melton as a cleaner. The job he had was hard and dangerous and during his time there he was badly crushed by buffers from an engine. He was fortunate to survive and spent several months in hospital recovering.

After the war, the problems at Melton continued to grow due to lack of investment, poor management and gradual decline in passenger traffic. Hewison, who became shedmaster at Melton in 1945, noted the difficulties he had with management coming from elsewhere and engine diagrams being ignored.[5] The track layout at Melton also did not help with no sidings beyond the platforms that could facilitate quick and easy movement of locomotives and trains. The sidings resulted in lots of dangerous activities, including fly shunting which meant drawing a wagon towards a set of facing points, releasing the engine from the vehicle whilst both in motion, letting the engine run ahead and then reversing the points so that the wagon overtakes the engine on a parallel track; the engine can then get behind the wagon and push it into place. Hewison forecast the dangers of this practice and an accident duly happened when a tank engine did not get far enough ahead and a wagon collided with one of its outside cylinders smashing it off the engine frame.[6]

Railway Families

Being a railway village, Melton saw generations of families working at the station or at the works. The company simply recruited the next generation in the village and youngsters found there were few alternative employers. The M & GN were also keen to attract skilled workers, the vast majority being between the ages of twenty and forty. While the houses they built were only let to married couples, lodgers supplemented their wages and the private housing in the village also provided accommodation. Unskilled staff who were employed at Melton tended not to be able to get houses in Melton as a result and lodged in adjacent villages. Half of the workforce who moved to Melton came from outside the county, the other half from elsewhere in Norfolk. What is clear is that the vast majority already had experience of working on the railways. Fifty percent of the workforce typically worked in the locomotive sheds and the others on the day-to-day running of the railway. One example of generational working at Melton is the family of Dick Fisher. He was a porter before the First World War but later became a guard serving the company until his retirement. Three of his five sons also spent their working lives with the railway. Len Bussey, in reflecting on his own experiences of working at Melton, started work at the station in 1934 at the M & GN works after passing an entrance examination. In this he said he was following in the footsteps of many in his family:

Like most "Meltonians", I was born into a railway family, my father Sydney was a Chargehand Boilersmith, my grandfather, Walter, a Signal Inspector, my uncle Horace, after servicing his apprenticeship left Melton Constable to go to London Kings Cross depot, and my uncle Matthew, after serving his apprenticeship left to enter the Royal Navy.[7]

Ray Meek followed in the family tradition by working at Melton. His grandfather, Fred, was a signalman and lived in a railway cottage at Hindolveston and walked the two and half miles to work and back every day until he moved into Melton itself. Violet, his daughter, worked in the offices and sons, Rowland and Cecil, also worked in the engineering and maintenance works. Cecil, upon completion of his apprenticeship had to find employment elsewhere and ended up at Leeds. Securing a post seems to have been aided by showing his certificate from Melton. Cecil eventually returned to Melton.[8]

Harold Drewey was the last station master at Melton Constable. Like many of his predecessors, and other staff at the station, his family had a long-standing connection with the railway. Harold was educated at Melton and then Fakenham Grammar School. He had a series of office-based jobs from the goods to the booking office. Drewey passed a series of exams to gain promotion and became station master at Gayton Road, then Thursford before ending up at Melton. Following the closure of the line, he became relief inspector in the region.[9]

Railway Institute

An important feature of a railwayman's life at Melton was the Railway Institute. It opened in 1896 for the exclusive use of company employees. The Institute contained a large hall where all forms of entertainment took place including public meetings. There were coffee and dining rooms, a reading room and library, which by 1920s, consisted of over 3,000 books. Books could be borrowed for a penny a week by family members up to the age of eighteen, and 2d per week for over 18s. It also organised bowls, chess, cricket, football and tennis clubs and teams. The Institute also had two Slipper Baths with constant hot water, still a luxury up to the 1930s. Apprentices developed their skills and knowledge at the Institute's evening classes.[10]

The former Railway Institute, Melton Constable, 2020.

I have memories of my grandparents talking about going up to the Institute for meetings and club activities. The Institute leisure activities were very much like working mens' clubs found in the North of England with the addition of providing an active community for learning.

Personal Experiences and Closure of the Station

My grandfather worked for nearly fifty years at Melton Constable, mainly as a wheeltapper until his retirement in 1961. Although his time at Melton was relatively quiet, he was responsible in 1930 for preventing a major accident. His role was to check on the wheels to ensure no cracks and he detected a faulty wheel on the express passing through Melton from Yarmouth. He successfully ensured the coach was detached and the train was able to continue its journey on to the Midlands.

My own experiences of Melton were from the late 1950s and early 1960s when it was on the decline. I do remember going via a train direct from Melton to Lowestoft which was where my other grandparents lived. But this route closed in the late 1950s. We then had to get the direct diesel train from Melton to Norwich Thorpe and then another train to Lowestoft. By the early 1960s, Melton was a route to nowhere. Lines had closed from Melton to Norwich City and west to Kings Lynn and the Midlands and east to Yarmouth. It became literally the end of the line and had little chance of survival against the swingeing cuts proposed by Dr. Beeching when the line from Sheringham to Melton closed in April 1964. The last passenger train left Melton on 4 April 1964. But at least successful lobbying ensured the line to Norwich from Sheringham was retained. Today, the line is a thriving one, often crowded in the summer, not only a route for holiday makers, but also, people working in Norwich or going on to London.

Legacy of the M & GN and Melton Constable today

Although Melton has been closed for over fifty years, the interest in the station and the M & GN line in general remains high. A thriving network of former employees and enthusiasts for the M & GN, the Circle, continue to meet and produce an excellent monthly bulletin and website. If one goes to Melton Constable today, although there are few signs of the old station, the Institute, now renamed the Country Club, continues and signs of the old station can still be seen around the village.

Spandrels from the old railway station are present today at the bus stop outside the former Hastings Arms public house. 'NCR' stands for Norfolk Central Railway, the name of the railway designated by the 1881 Amalgamation Act before further amalgamation created the M & GN.

Notes

1 *M & GN Circle Newsletter: Circle 430/13.*

2 *Marriott (1974) p.6.*

3 *Ibid. p.8.*

4 *Ibid. p.9.*

5 *Hewison (1981).*

6 *Ibid.*

7 *M & GN Circle Bulletin, 306/9.*

8 *Raymond Meek talks about his village and family, M & GNRailway Society no.3.*

9 *Harold Drewry and Alan Bullen—Starting on the railway, M & GNRailway Society no.3.*

10 *http://norfolk-orbital-railway.co.uk/audio-railway-institute-melton-constable/*

Harwich: The Gateway To The Continent

One of the places that I continually heard a lot about during my childhood as a railway hub was Harwich and Parkeston. Harwich is a historic port on the north east tip of the Essex coastline and, from the 17th century, has been an important starting point for ships going across the North Sea. Parkeston Quay, just further up the estuary, later became the terminal for ferries and cargo ships to the continent. I have always seen Harwich and Parkeston to be the symbol of the 'romantic' period of rail travel and as a very important place of railway employment. I am aware many railway workers who worked alongside my father were based at Parkeston for a number of years. Also, my late brother in law was a British Transport Policeman based there for a number of years.

This chapter outlines how Harwich and Parkeston Quay (now renamed Harwich International) evolved as key railway stations exemplified by reminiscences of various workers who worked on the line to Manningtree and beyond.

Emergence of Harwich as a Railway Terminus

Harwich had, from the 17th century, been an important port for mail and passengers traffic to the continent. But it suffered from competition with the Dover to Calais service especially when a decision was made to transfer all continental mail via London. Once railway lines started to appear in East Anglia in the 1840s, discussions emerged as to where and how a line could be built to enable ferry links to the continent. Ipswich was a possibility as it had steamer links to the Netherlands.

A guidebook issued by the Great Eastern Railway for German tourists travelling by way of the Hook of Holland to Parkeston Quay route. On the cover is an illustration of London's Liverpool Street Station.

The original railway station at Harwich, from which passengers had to walk to the pier from where the continental steamers sailed.

However, due to pressure from local councils in North Essex, an Act was secured in 1847 for a line from the south bank of the Stour from Manningtree to Harwich. Delays occurred as raising the finance was no easy undertaking, and competition between two main railway companies, ECR and EUR caused friction. The ECR eventually won; the line being completed and opened in 1854.

There was an assumption that the opening up of the railway line and the development of the port would be, as the *Illustrated London News* said at the time, 'a day of promise for the people of Harwich, who are looking forward to great things from this line, and the north of Europe steamers which are shortly to be put on the station'.[1]

Alongside the railway line, preparations were being made for steamship services to and from Harwich. This led to the GER beginning to operate a weekly cargo service from Harwich to Rotterdam in 1863. By the early 1870s a continental express between London and Harwich was making the journey in just under two hours.

The expansion was aided by two major developments. The first was the creation of a new port two miles upriver at Parkeston, enabling much larger ships to dock, and on the Dutch side, the completion of a new waterway making Rotterdam accessible at any tide. Even more important was the opening of the Hook of Holland, which became, in 1904, the main terminal for ferries from Harwich. The construction of Parkeston meant that Harwich station lost a great

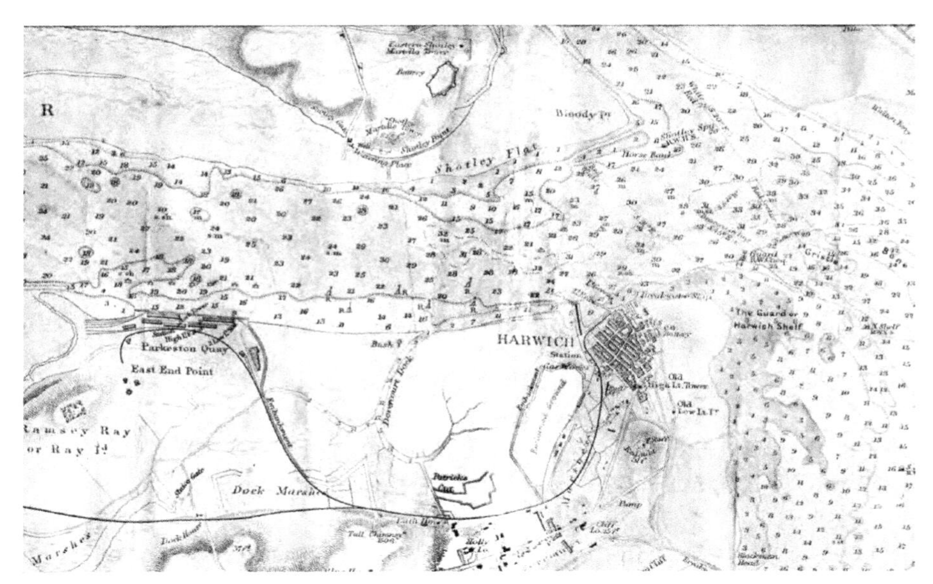

Parkeston Quay seen on a chart published about 1890.

deal of traffic. The station at Harwich originally had three platforms with lines which ran directly onto two piers from which the GER ferry services operated. The lines down the piers became redundant and the station, whilst remaining the terminus of the line from Manningtree, took on a less important role than Parkeston.

Parkeston Quay as the Port for Ferries

The creation of Parkeston Quay was a major engineering undertaking and necessitated the reclaiming of marsh land. Work began in 1874 but it was not until 1883 that the new quay was formally opened. It was originally called 'Stour Quay'. This was later changed to Harwich (Parkeston) Quay, named after Charles H. Parkes, Chairman of the GER. To support the needs of the Quay, a small community of workers' houses was established. In a similar way to Melton Constable, the company owned the majority of the houses which were only available to railway workers. There were also three grander houses for the Station Master, the Port Manager and the Marine Superintendent.

Like Melton, Parkeston developed an economic, social and cultural infrastructure to support the community. This included, in 1887, a Wesleyan Chapel and St. Gabriel's, an iron church known locally as the 'The Tin Tabernacle'. A third and much larger church, St.Paul's, was built in 1914. A series of shops opened, including a Co-op in 1897. The Co-op not only provided butchery, grocery and drapery stores, but also a meeting room which also acted as a library.[2]

The GER started a regular service between Antwerp and Harwich in 1864 but it was the creation of the new quay at Parkeston that brought about a major expansion of ferry services. The Royal Danish Mail Service began a service from Esbjerg in 1880 and this was transferred to Parkeston in 1882. Others followed, with services from Parkeston to Hamburg, Germany, in 1884 and in 1910 to Sweden.

Growth of Harwich and Surrounding Area

One consequence of Parkeston developing as a railway centre, was that Harwich, and the adjacent town of Dovercourt grew in size with new industries and, the latter, as a holiday centre. Both towns doubled their populations between 1851 and the beginning of the 20th century. The popularity of the area with day visitors and holiday-makers was noted in 1899, 'a fashionable and delightful seaside resort has grown'.[3] Harwich was also a significant fishing port at this time, with over 250 men being employed in this industry by the outbreak of the First World War. There were not only regular passenger services to the Netherlands, but also coastal paddle steamers between Harwich, Ipswich and Felixstowe in the summer months. The railways provided easy access to a coastal trip either for the day or as a base for a longer holiday.

Such growth was not maintained in the 1920s. The worldwide economic depression hit Harwich and the surrounding area hard. Both passenger and freight ferries suffered and the fishing industry was reduced to a few shrimp boats.

Only after 1960 did the area begin to revive with the opening of a new terminal for car ferries, and the later introduction of containers for freight.

Parkeston Quay as a Railway Centre

The creation of the quay at Parkeston led, by the end of the 19th century, to the area becoming a major railway centre housing locomotives with supporting workforce.

By 1900, Parkeston provided, in addition to a quay capable of berthing seven ships, a hotel, a locomotive depot, five miles of railway sidings and lines to serve the local refineries as well as a tip-site for an aggregates company.

For much of the 20th century, the focus of the Quay was its interconnectedness with the railway station. The vast majority of passengers were foot passengers and, to accommodate the sheer volume of traffic and people, a separate station, Parkeston Quay West, operated for the daily service to the Hook of Holland.

Between the wars, it became an increasingly significant railway centre with large engine sheds for repairs and turntables; by 1923, for example, it was the

Parkeston Quay station in 1950s.

base for over 120 steam engines.

The drivers and the firemen for the boat trains were all based at Parkeston Quay and it was regarded as a prestigious route, despite being called 'the stiffest locomotive duty over any part of the old Great Eastern system'.[4]

By the mid- to late-1950s the number of steam locomotives had declined. Ian Allan's *Locoshed Book* listed just twenty-four on 11 May 1957. The numbers of shunting and tank engines had been reduced as diesel-powered units and diesel multiple units had begun to work local services. Overall, there remained 33 units allocated to the shed in 1959, but by 1967 the facility had been demolished.

The demolition of the locomotive shed allowed the construction of the new Freightliner terminal on the site, which opened in May 1968.

The Boat Train

Although there were regular services on the line between Harwich and Manningtree with connections to Ipswich or Colchester, it was the boat trains that were the mainstay of the line. They began in 1882 and from 1897 were run as two separate trains, the *Hook of Holland* and the *Antwerp Express*.

There were further coach improvements in 1904, which meant there were new carriages and vestibules throughout together with restaurant cars, and transfer facilities at Parkeston Quay were excellent. This secured for the Great Eastern Railway a reputation for providing the most comfortable journey to the continent. These trains were the first to be fitted with a new steam system of heating for passengers. The success of the new facilities meant that, the following year, dining cars were introduced on the *Antwerp Boat Express*. In 1906, similar facilities were included on the boat trains from the north to Parkeston. The reputation of these trains, with three dining cars, became a major marketing success for the company and its ferries.[5]

The services quickly became very popular. In 1911, the GER Magazine noted that it was possible to get a ticket all the way from Harwich, via the Hook of Holland, to Vladivostok on the *Trans-Siberian Express*.[6] Before the outbreak of war in 1914, services opened up to Hamburg and Gothenburg but they were not to survive the conflict. Another successful service was to Esbjerg in Denmark, which not only included passengers but pigs and other animals. The importance of the port and the ferry services to the local area was substantial and by 1914 the GER was the largest employer in Harwich.

During the inter-war period, the boat trains from London to Harwich remained very popular and working on them was regarded as challenging, but worthwhile. It was seen as a job for experienced drivers and firemen. Timekeeping was critical with the connections to the ferries and the arrival and turnaround at Harwich requiring considerable skill.[7] The Express with Pullman style seating was luxurious particularly for first class passengers in their two carriages. In addition, there were two dining cars, one for first class and one for second.

The skill with which the driver and the fireman completed the journey to Harwich, and what they had to do upon arrival in preparation for the following day, can be seen from the following commentary on travelling on the Express upon arrival at the port:

> No time is to be wasted here, as the Antwerp train is due in 10 minutes behind us, and before that our passengers must be off the platform. A shunting engine has whisked off the two vans at the rear and taken them round on to the Quay itself, opposite the Hook of Holland steamer, and our engine and train have moved off to the carriage sidings.[8]

At the end of the First World War, there was a surplus of train ferries—boats that had track on them and could include carriages. Harwich seemed an obvious place to start a service using these train ferries rather than Parkeston because of the proximity of the line to the shoreline. With support from companies in Belgium, the *Great Eastern Train Ferry Company* was formed and the first train ferry service opened to Zeebrugge in 1924. Three ferries were introduced and continued in service up to the outbreak of war in 1939. During the war they were commissioned for war work. Two were destroyed during the war, but one, renamed the *Essex Ferry*, began work again across the North Sea in 1946.

Train Ferry leaving Harwich.

A replacement ship commenced operation in 1955 and this boat carried 38 railway carriages and accommodation for twelve passengers, surviving in service until 1981.[9] Another ferry, the *Suffolk Ferry* had begun in service in 1947 and continued operating until 1980. The third boat, the *Norfolk Ferry* entered service, using the same route in 1951, and operated until 1972. The fourth was the *Cambridge Ferry* which began in 1964 also operating the same route. Towards the latter part of their service, some of these ferries were used on a Harwich to Dunkirk route. From the 1960s to the 1980s, a range of other ferry craft were used, including the *Speedlink Vanguard*. This ship was involved in a major accident in December 1982, when it collided with Townsend Thoresen's roll on, roll off ferry *European Gateway* two miles off Harwich. Unfortunately, two lorry drivers died. The incident made headlines for the ways in which the local population of Harwich came to the rescue. The local paper reported that 'the individual acts of heroism are too numerous to mention'.[10]

Although the ferry returned to service, it was clear that, during the 1980s, the service was no longer financially viable. The final train ferry service ran in 1987.

The other services from Parkeston continued and there were still cross-country services to the ferry terminus up to the 1980s. Even as late as 1985, there was the *European* running to Harwich from Manchester Victoria. Although this service did not last long, some form of long-distance service remained until 1991.

To many people Harwich was the gateway to the continent. Posters and leaflets between the wars and into the 1950s and 60s promoted this romantic mode of travel.

The Prinz Hamlet leaves Harwich for the German port of Hamburg, 1980.

For many families, such trips were a great new adventure, as can be seen from these words from a young girl on her first trip abroad:

> On our overnight crossing to Holland I was so excited, what an adventure this was going to be. The furthest we had been before was to Butlins in Skegness. I lay in my bunk puzzling at the hook on the wall at the side of my head. It was covered in red velvet at the top of a 2-inch circle of padded velvet. Whatever was its purpose? Next morning my curiosity got the better of me and I asked a member of the crew who said it was for hanging a pocket watch on. Simple really![11]

Decline of Ferry Services

As modes of transport changed from the 1960s onwards, particularly with the growth of cheaper air travel, the boat trains and ferry services began to decline in popularity. From transporting one million plus passengers, the ferry service to the continent today consists of twice daily sailings to the Hook of Holland.

From 1995 Parkeston Quay station was renamed Harwich International. It was all part of a re-branding of the station following major developments and the opening of a new passenger terminal in the same year.

The changing role of the railway line from Harwich to Manningtree can be seen in a decline of direct services to London and an increase of local services. This was made possible by electrification of the line in 1986 and the subsequent re-branding of the line to the Mayflower line.

Mayflower Line

Today the line thrives with regular services between Harwich and Manningtree—all connecting to London by mainline trains. There are still some occasional through trains. The line is also popular with the local population, providing a quick and easy way to Colchester or London. It has also become important again as a tourist line with the increasing marketing of Harwich itself as an important historical port town. The line remains well served by regular freight services.

Notes

1 *Weaver (1975) p.135.*

2 *http://www.harwichanddovercourt.co.uk/parkeston-life/*

3 *Quoted in Weaver (1975) p.148.*

4 *https://www.railwaywondersoftheworld.com/hook_holland.html*

5 *https://www.railwaywondersoftheworld.com/hook_holland.html)*

6 *GER 1.2.*

7 *https://www.railwaywondersoftheworld.com/hook_holland.html*

8 *https://www.railwaywondersoftheworld.com/hook_holland.html*

9 *http://www.harwichanddovercourt.co.uk/train-ferry-service/*

10 *http://www.harwichanddovercourt.co.uk/train-ferry-service/*

11 *https://www.culture24.org.uk/history-and-heritage/transport-and-industry/art76166*

Impact of the Second World War

This chapter reviews the impact of the Second World War on the railways of East Anglia. There are several reasons why this specific period has a distinct chapter. The war had a major role in revitalising some local rural lines, which were used to move materials for the construction of aerodromes, and later fuel. The region hosted the huge number of aerodromes, built to enable bombing raids, and other air-borne operations, into continental Europe by British and American forces. Many lines were almost totally taken over for war-related transport, in particular freight and related services. They also became the main means of transport around the region for those working in the armed forces, providing them access to the rest of the country. The war had a direct impact on some stations in terms of bombing, most notably Norwich City.

Initial Impact on the Railways of East Anglia

After the initial curtailment of passenger services on the outbreak of war, there was, by the middle of 1940, increased traffic with more passengers on all lines what with the movement of troops, armaments and petrol rationing curtailing road transportation. One of the most challenging shifts, for drivers and firemen, were freight trains carrying petrol. Petrol for commercial and military use had to come across country and the railway network was the only means to move significant quantities whether it be aircraft fuel or to diesel to power warships.

Moving of tanks by train.

At first, East Anglia rural villages were seen as a safe destination for many children from London. In early September 1939, the first evacuee trains left London for Ipswich, Colchester, Cambridge, Bury St. Edmunds and Norwich. At each station there were official receptions for the boys and girls. As Brown states:

> On the first day, the whole operation went quite smoothly. The first party of about one thousand arriving at Norwich were settled into villages

during the afternoon. Colchester moved two trainloads to their new homes by early afternoon.[1]

Evacuees leaving Cromer station in June 1940. Following the fall of France, a second wave of evacuation took place from the coastal towns in southern and eastern England that faced German-controlled areas of Europe.

However, the following day, the welcoming parties found far fewer unaccompanied children with the majority being expectant mothers with young children. The reason was that many families in the East End of London had, for the time being, decided to stay put. By June 1940, it was children from East Anglian coastal towns such as Cromer, Great Yarmouth and Lowestoft that were being evacuated by train to rural Derbyshire, Nottinghamshire and Wales in response to the capitulation of France and the increased likelihood of invasion from the continent.

Transporting materials for airfield construction became one of the major tasks of the railways from 1940 onwards. In 1942, six trains a day were allocated to take rubble from around the country to East Anglia. This was increased to nine per day the following year with additional trains for bricks and building materials. Train loads of bomb debris from London were transported into sidings across the region, with some of the smaller branch lines at long last coming into their own. Lines like the mid-Suffolk and small branches to Hadleigh, Eye and Framlingham became logistical routes to the new airfields where that rubble was used as hard-core.

Travelling by train could often end up being much longer with delays, not only due to troop movements, which had priority, but the impact of bombing on stations and lines. E.J. Rudsdale's trip to London from Colchester at the end of August in 1940 is described:

> I decided to catch the 5.35 to London but found it had been cancelled. The next was the 6.13 but at 6 o'clock there was another alarm and all passengers were made to shelter in the new subways. The London train came in and crawled along at 15mph as far as Ingatestone, where 'all clear' was given and finally got to Liverpool Street at 8.30.[2]

Such hazards were almost daily and his return trip to Colchester the following day was equally eventful:

> At Liverpool Street we found a notice to say that all passengers beyond Brentwood must change there as there was an unexploded bomb on the main line. Apparently, it was there last night when I came through but had not been noticed. This meant that after travelling in acute discomfort we were compelled to take buses from Brentwood to Shenfield station… I noticed that a German 'plane was brought down right across the railway line near Shenfield. … The train to Colchester was packed, mostly with soldiers…[3]

Daily Lives of Railway Workers and their Families

Life for railwaymen during the war was challenging at the best of times. They often had to work very long hours. Robertson, in his volume on memories of working on the railways during the war, points out that the sheer pressure when driving a train took its toll and he had to retire from the footplate due to exhaustion and stress.[4] Trains were delayed due to bombing raids elsewhere or, if there was an urgent shipment that took priority. Footplatemen also had to ensure their fireboxes were not open when moving, in case they were seen by enemy aircraft.

For many railway families, the war meant moving to a new town or village, as some employees had joined the armed forces or the company needed to increase the workforce at particular places. My own parents moved in 1942 from Melton Constable to Sudbury as a result of such demands. My father was now a fireman and, during the war, Sudbury became a key centre for the movement of freight and goods for the nearby airfield and required additional personnel.

Peter Hall, the theatre and film director, was the son of a railwayman and was born and brought up in Suffolk. His father, before the war, was a 'miserably paid clerk in the goods depot at Bury St. Edmunds station'.[5] In the late 1930s the family moved to Barnham, a small station between Thetford and Bury, where Peter's father became station master. Typical of many rural stations in East Anglia at this time, it was rather a sleepy and quiet place, with a signal box and goods sidings having but two trains each way per day and one goods train passing through. In addition to the station master, there was also a signalman, a junior clerk and an odd-job man. As Hall describes in his autobiography, many of the railwaymen at this time were more like Edwardian gentlemen, impeccably turned out, with big moustaches, stiff white collars and gold chains attached to their pocket watches.[6]

This gentle lifestyle was shattered when, just before the war, his father secured promotion to be relief station master. He had to be available to go anywhere in East Anglia when men were sick or on holiday. During the war his father moved up another level and became station master at Shelford, on the main line between Cambridge to London. Like most station masters, the family lived in a house alongside the station. It was 'basic' and was attached to the station booking hall.

Railway Home Guard in training.

Like other workers employed on the 'home front', railway workers also had to join their Home Guard unit. Railwaymen, in the larger towns and cities, formed there own specialist Railway Home Guard platoons. One of these was at Ipswich where Peter Middleton, in his recollections, recalls how he had to learn to put trains out of action in the event of an invasion. They were also trained to identify potential spies that might be travelling by train.[7]

The demands of war, both in terms of movement of goods and passengers, were often too much for the railway system and inefficiencies crept in.

Tragic Incidents

Simple issues such as drivers and firemen locating their engines during blackouts presented unexpected hazards. Trains, inevitably, were easy targets for enemy aircraft. Rudsdale, in his journals refers to one incident in January 1941 when a passenger train from London to Ipswich was bombed and machine gunned at Colchester and the guard was killed:

> ... a German plane, flying in a thick snowstorm, dropped 4 bombs near the London-Yarmouth train as it passed Chitt's Hill (on the approach to Colchester North station). All missed but he opened fire and broke many windows, hitting six people.[8]

Every journey might produce unseen hazards that were not there a few minutes ago. In 1943, a train from London to Harwich fell into a hole blown in the embankment between Shenfield and Ingatestone and the driver and the fireman, both Harwich men, were killed.[9]

Of all the numerous incidents across East Anglia, the most famous was at Soham with an ammunition train. A goods train was travelling across East Anglia from Whitemoor in Cambridgeshire to Goodmayes yard and had been diverted to go via Ely. The driver was Benjamin Gimbert, with James Nightall as the fireman. The train cargo was high explosive bombs. Passing the signal for Soham, the driver suddenly noticed the wagon behind the engine was on

Soham railway disaster.

fire. Sending a whistle signal to the guard, the driver stopped the train on the up main line at the far end of the station. Fireman Nightall uncoupled the first wagon from the train. Their plan was for the driver to move the locomotive with wagon that was on fire clear of the station and the village before de-coupling it from the engine. They stopped by the signalbox to inform the signalman what they were doing. Just as the signalman was coming down the steps of the box, the wagon exploded demolishing the signal box and causing enormous damage to many of the nearby houses. Nightall was killed, and driver Gimbert seriously injured. The signalman was to die the same day. The driver and fireman were awarded the George Cross for their bravery, Nightall posthumously. In another fitting tribute for both men, they had engines named after them.[10]

Impact of War on Families and Places of Work

For many families, including my own, the wartime meant living from one day to the next and hoping their loved ones would not get caught up in accidents or bombings. Both my parents had to deal with sudden changes. My mother worked for a while in Norwich and commuted from Melton Constable. My father worked at Melton, dealing with last minute changes to his work.

Although their lives became easier when they moved to Sudbury, they still had to cope with uncertainly—the fear of raids or sudden shift changes in response to needs of nearby aerodromes. This uncertainty meant that going to see relatives elsewhere in the region was very difficult. Letters were the only form of communication as most people did not have access to a telephone.

Women railway workers relaying track.

The war also meant that women took on jobs that had previously been the preserve of men—handling parcels and merchandise at stations, booking clerks, ticket collectors and cleaners.[11] Mary Purcell, who worked as a clerk on the M & GN line, referred to the wide variety of goods she had to manage, including 'birds, fowl, etc., tied by their legs with a label on, with their destination'.[12] With time however, as more men joined the armed forces, women took on the more physical occupations. This included tasks such as replacing track as platelayers.

For the vast majority of railway workers, both men and women, the war was a period of non-stop work with very few opportunities for leisure. As Reg Robertson says in his memoirs on working on the Eastern region during the war, 'There was no getting together at weekends with friends or families when most people were free'.[13] He also states that the wartime reinforced divisions within the workforce—between the foremen and supervisors, and the rest. The stark reality of what they saw and experienced during this period comes to life in this account from Robertson:

> We had just left Stratford on the down line and the next stop was Ilford…It was midday. [Approaching Forest Gate], the station suddenly disappeared. Our view between the concrete walls of the cutting was nothing but grey dust and black smoke. My mate made an emergency stop and as the haze cleared, we saw that a rocket had exploded in the street to the right of the station.[14]

With the demands of transporting wounded soldiers around the country, many drivers and firemen had to suddenly go and work in other regions. This particularly increased after the 1944 D-Day landings when some trains were specifically designated to be used as ambulance trains.[15]

Despite the war meaning an increased use of the railways there were few, if any, improvements to the quality of either the locomotives or the passenger rolling stock. Although the network was brought under government control, there was no major investment or planning for the post-war period. These failures had a particular impact on the railways of East Anglia. Many of the smaller rural lines' demise was inevitable.

Notes

1 *Brown (1980) p.169.*

2 *Pearson (2010) p.18.*

3 *Ibid. p.19.*

4 *Robertson (1996).*

5 *Hall (2000).*

6 *Ibid.*

7 *Middleton (n.d.) Oral History Recording 2001, National Railway Museum, York, National Archive of Railway Oral History (NAROH).*

8 *Pearson (2010) p.58.*

9 *Freestone and Smith (1998) pp.133-4.*

10 *see Andrew Dow in Steam World, 2005 (221) p.28, Locomotive Magazine. 1944, 50, p.180, Wragg (2012) p.141.)*

11 *Simialr roles had been taken on by women during World War I.*

12 *Major (2018) p.114.)*

13 *Robertson (1996) p.14.*

14 *Ibid. p.147.*

15 *Smith (1946) 44th USA Ambulance Train, LNER Railway Magazine, February, reprinted in Joint Line, no.185 p.46-7.*

The Britannia Class

Like many children during the 1950s I became a train spotter. It was perhaps inevitable that I should be fascinated with identifying and spotting particular locomotives given my family background and the fact I was regularly travelling by train. While this phase only lasted for a few years (I think I could say I had grown out of it by the time I became a teenager) I do have fond memories of spending several happy hours looking for specific engines at Colchester or Ipswich. The engines I always looked out for were the pride of the Eastern Region, the Britannia class.

Those memories form the focus of this chapter, which, is the only chapter that looks specifically at locomotives. Not only does it bring back personal memories, more significantly it is this class of locomotives that people who worked on the railways recall most fondly.

The Britannia class of locomotives was built at Crewe, the first one being named *Britannia*. Fifty four more locomotives followed, built to the same design. They were the first locomotives built under the nationalised *British Railways* coming into service in 1951.

The Britannias had a major impact on train services and the lives of the drivers and firemen. They became the flagship locomotives for the Eastern Region. They were much bigger and more powerful than other locomotives used in the Region. Twenty-three were allocated to run on the main line from London to Norwich. Big and powerful, they were very heavy on coal but had the advantage of being able to use poorer quality coal than other locomotives.

Many of the Britannia class had names from British history that indicated a sense of "power and greatness"—names such as *John Bunyan, William Shakespeare, Oliver Cromwell, Owen Glendower, Robin Hood, Boadicea, Robert Burns, Coeur-de-Lion, John of Gaunt* and *Alfred the Great*. Later engine names inspired a sense of speed or made connections to Roman deities. They included *Apollo, Mercury, Venus, Tornado, Arrow* and *Lightning*. Several had names with the suffix "star" such as *Morning Star, Western Star, Polar Star* and *Rising Star*. The final group of locomotives, which came into service in 1954, were named after Scottish estuaries such as *Solway Firth, Firth of Clyde* and *Moray Firth*.

The *Britannia* locomotive itself was initially based at Stratford, the main depot for the Eastern Region trains out of London. It was at first used to haul express trains to Norwich and Yarmouth but later became used for the boat trains to Harwich. From 1959 to 1961 it was based at Norwich, and later still at March, before finally being based in the London Midland Region, until it was withdrawn in 1966.[1]

The locomotive pulled King George VI's funeral train for the journey between Kings Lynn and London in February 1952. Its cab and carriage roofs were conspicuously painted white and the body of the train black, with the King's coat of arms centred on each carriage side.[2]

During 1951 and 1952, the Britannia class often hauled *The Norfolkman* or *The East Anglian* express services between London and Norwich. When it began hauling the boat trains to Harwich, it tended to be based at Parkeston. My first sighting of the famous engine class was at Colchester, during a run in the late 1950s, as the *Essex Coast Express* from London to Clacton.

The success and subsequent iconic status of the Britannia class was that it brought together, in one locomotive, some of the most effective design features found in a number of other engines during this period.[3]

The class had a very distinctive livery, Brunswick green being chosen for all express engines. A unique feature of the Britannias was that this green was lined with orange and black piping. They also had brass name plates.

Memories of Working and Maintaining the Britannia Class

While the class was well liked by crews in most regions of British Railways, those operating them from Stratford found their low weight and highly transformed motor power was particularly suited to the geography of East Anglia.[4]

Railwaymen who worked with the locomotive felt it was both reliable and a good workhorse. Bill Harvey remembers working with the class as a locomotive shed master and dedicates a special chapter to the locomotive.[5] He singles out the period 1951-1961, when the Britannia class was at Norwich, as the crowning years of his career. The distinctive look, with smoke deflectors, speed, and power were simply impressive. He points out their reliability and the low cost of maintaining their axleboxes. Only one, based at Norwich, ever needed its original bearings replaced despite their heavy use.[6]

Harvey says that over a period of ten years, the original eight locomotives allocated to Norwich, nos 70006-13, accumulated some 5,806,919 miles. Each of the locomotives that he was responsible for achieved around 700,000 mileage.

A Britannia class could haul an eleven-coach train from Norwich to London in two hours. With this speed, a crew could often make the journey from Norwich to London via Ipswich, and back to Cambridge within a shift.

British Railways inspired personal investment in the locomotives by allowing the driver's name to be attached to the side of his cab. As George Ewles noted:

> When a man reached this position, he didn't think so much that we worked for the railway; he was so proud he thought he owned it.[7]

Wear and tear eventually took their toll on the class and the Britannias were replaced by diesel electric. By 1961 only sixteen remained operational and by the end of the year diesels had taken over completely.

Britannia and Heritage Lines

Unfortunately, only two of the Britannia class survive to be used for heritage lines and rail tours—the *Britannia* (the prototype) and *Oliver Cromwell.*

Initially it was planned that *Britannia* would form part of the National Railway Collection at the National Railway Museum at York, but the museum chose to preserve 70013, *Oliver Cromwell,* instead.

It is said that *Britannia* was not chosen because of its prototype design and there were distinct construction differences compared with other members of the class. Some considered this would make its preservation more complicated. Others argue that *Britannia* was in a poor mechanical condition. It's true to say that *Britannia* had numerous problems during its time with British Railways.

After several owners, it ended up at Severn Valley Heritage railway in a non-operational state. In 1980 it moved to the Nene Valley railway staying there until the year 2000. During this time it did become operational. From 2000 onwards, in need of urgent and costly repairs, it was eventually bought by the Royal Scot Locomotive and General Trust. It has subsequently been used for occasional excursion even returning to the Severn Valley under a new green rather than standard black livery.

I remember seeing the *Britannia* in 2012 when it passed through Colchester and Manningtree on a special excursion to Norwich. It looked superb with its green livery. Its passing through Colchester was captured on film and the crowds that watched along the line are a testament to the locomotive's popularity in the 21st century.[8]

The *Oliver Cromwell* became based at the National Railway Museum. It was used to conduct special rail-tours and was last seen in the region at the re-opening of the link from the *North Norfolk Railway* to the main line at Sheringham in 2010. It was withdrawn from service in December 2018 and is awaiting major refurbishment under the supervision of the Grand Central

70013 Oliver Cromwell approaching Weybourne on the North Norfolk Railway, 11 March 2010.

Railway at Loughborough.

Notes

1 *see http://www.davidheyscollection.com/page91.htm for more detail on the journey of the Britannia.*

2 *Watling (2020) The Funeral Carriage—GNR Saloon no.6, Great Eastern Journal,19.2,issue no 182, p.14-16.*

3 *https://preservedbritishsteamlocomotives.com/7p6f-70000-70054-4-6-2-br-standard-britannia/*

4 *https://preservedbritishsteamlocomotives.com/7p6f-70000-70054-4-6-2-br-standard-britannia/*

5 *Harvey (1986).*

6 *Ibid. p.180.*

7 *Brodribb (2009) p.250.*

8 *https://youtu.be/L2EbDSUQcqs*

From Steam to Diesel and Electric

Many volumes on the history of the railways tend to concentrate on the steam era. However, one of the most important changes within the history of the railways was the move from steam to diesel and electric in the 1950s and 1960s. This move improved the efficiency of the railway system as trains were now more likely to run to time. It also helped the environment. No longer were areas around stations and railway lines constantly full of smoke and soot. Most important of all, the change radically improved the quality of life for railway workers. From having to retire early due to lung problems, railway workers could now look forward to a longer healthier life and enjoy their retirement. Their working conditions were also much better. No longer would they be exposed to the elements of the weather. They would now be enclosed in warm cabs with proper heating systems. Modernisation came with a cost—a drastic reduction in the workforce throughout the country and this had a dramatic effect in East Anglia.

This chapter outlines how the transfer from steam to diesel and electric took place in East Anglia and the impact it had on the workforce.

Although the railways were nationalised in 1948, it was nearly a decade before major changes could be seen. The transfer from steam to diesel and electric took place in the Eastern Region in the 1950s and 1960s. The shift presented major issues for the workforce, the support infrastructure and the day-to-day management of the lines. Under steam, a large workforce was needed to support the running of every train. Coal and water had to be easily available and ready for instant use getting each engine prepared for the day's journeys. Even moving a locomotive from one track to another took time. Turntables were needed and timekeeping was difficult to maintain. With the change to diesel and electric, equipment and many jobs were no longer required. Firemen were no longer required and there was no need to have depots at regular intervals for refuelling the locomotives. The impact of the changes necessitated re-skilling the drivers from steam to diesel and electric.

Modernisation Plan

In 1955, British Railways launched its Modernisation plan with the aim of electrifying mainline routes and introducing a streamlined system with diesel powered locomotives. The plan in the Eastern Region began with the extension of overhead wires beyond Chelmsford to Ipswich and on the lines to Clacton and Walton, Harwich and Felixstowe. A re-think at the end of 1959 resulted in deferring electrification beyond Colchester. However electrification had already been agreed for suburban lines to Clacton and Walton and the new service started in March 1959. It took until the 1980s, following the oil crisis of the previous decade, that electrification from Colchester to Ipswich and Norwich took place. Lines to Braintree from Witham and Harwich to Manningtree were also electrified during this period.

Four different types of motor power were introduced. First were the diesel electric locomotives that began to appear in the region in 1957 and 1958. Here there were two main types: Brush Electrics, and the more powerful English Electric. They were much quicker than steam locomotives and did not need to be turned around at terminal points. This meant that services could be increased and, of course, were much cheaper to run than coal and steam powered locomotives. Compared with the Britannia steam locomotives, these English Electric engines could pull more carriages and still match the speed. The second type were diesel multiple units usually with two carriages. Their introduction in the region began in Norfolk on local branch lines in 1955 but gradually extended across the region.

Diesel electric hauled train, Class 31 D5520 at Colchester.

The third and fourth types required overhead electric wires and were either electric powered locomotives or electric powered units. Electrically powered units had gradually been introduced out of London Liverpool Street in the 1950s reaching Chelmsford in the summer of 1956 and, by the end of that year, as far as Southend.

For the Eastern Region, it was the diesel locomotives and the diesel multiple units that were the most visible signs of the change. Electric powered units were first used on the Clacton and Walton lines.[1]

The introduction of these new engines and units meant training was needed and the introduction of single driver trains was only achieved after lengthy negotiations with the trade unions.

It was anticipated that the Eastern Region would have, by 1963, approximately 400 main line diesel locomotives. There would also be 180 diesel multiple units and 369 electrical units.

1959 was the big year of change from steam to diesel and electric in the Eastern Region. Figures for that year give an indication of the changes taking place:

- 26 high powered diesel electric locomotives
- 96 diesel multiple units
- 124 electrically powered sets
- 22 Britannia classed steam locomotives.

Passenger train mileage in that year was 39.6% powered by diesel, 38.9% by steam and 21.5% by electric.[2]

Passengers benefited from not only a cleaner and smoother rail journey but a more regular efficient service. The aim was to have the timetable arranged in such a way that a passenger anywhere in East Anglia could have at least an hourly service to their initial destination.

The speed of change was swift. For example, on 2 November 1959 Ipswich Motive Power Depot changed from steam to diesel completely. This was the first mainline steam motive power depot in the country to change to diesel for both passenger and freight services. Twenty-seven mainline diesel-electric locomotives were allocated to the depot to replace the 60 steam locomotives. Between twenty and thirty diesel shunting locomotives were also maintained at Ipswich. This changeover alone involved the conversion of over 200 drivers from steam to diesel, with significant re-training for maintenance staff. Diesel locomotive working at Ipswich in the late 1950s and early 1960s covered passenger and freight train services between Yarmouth, Lowestoft, Ipswich and London, as well as cross-country services between Ipswich and Peterborough and freight services to March and beyond.[3]

Ipswich was, as Allan states, 'the centre of great diesel activity' with hourly services to Felixstowe and also on the East Suffolk line to Lowestoft. Any retention of steam locomotives in the area was seen as short-term and mainly for freight.[4]

On the main lines, such as Ipswich to Norwich and Ipswich to London, English Electric locomotives replaced the Britannia class. On local and branch lines, such as Ipswich to Felixstowe and Ipswich to Lowestoft, diesel multiple units were introduced.

The gradual development of electrically powered units was linked to the electrification of the line from Colchester to Clacton and Walton. The line already had overhead power to Southend and Colchester.

There had already been evidence of increased use on the lines to Shenfield and Chelmsford as a result of electrification. Trains were now much more reliable, there were more of them, and they were much more comfortable than the earlier steam hauled carriages. The evidence from 1958, for example, showed passenger numbers and takings had more than doubled since the last years of steam.

Diesel Multiple Units (DMUs)

The most familiar train to be seen on local lines in East Anglia from the mid-1950s onwards were the diesel multiple units. These are the trains I was most familiar with, as they were the mainstay of the Stour Valley branch where my father was one of the drivers. He found the trains fine to drive, fairly straightforward and usually reliable. Whilst they lasted much longer than they should have, into the 1980s, and sometimes could make too much noise, they did what was required in getting passengers to their destinations, usually on time.

These DMUs or diesel railcars, as they became known, were economical compared with steam. They only needed a driver and a guard to run. In time the guards became responsible for collecting tickets. This led to the closure of some small ticket offices.

Diesel multiple unit in 1960s. The driver of this train is the author's father, Ernest Bourn.

Prior to the Beeching Axe in the 1960s, there had already been some major rationalisation and closure of local lines in East Anglia. In 1955 a survey had been undertaken across a range of routes to assess the true nature of revenue and costs. Initially the survey was focused on steam trains but it was repeated with diesel railcars with the results then compared. What the surveys showed was that stopping trains on local lines were poorly served apart from summertime. The original surveys showed that where railcar operations had begun there were noticeable improvements, it was much cheaper to run and more efficient. Once railcars were generally introduced, the results were very positive. Passenger numbers increased, trains were quicker and much cleaner. These trains helped justify keeping some lines open when threatened with imminent closure although not from the Beeching axe when it fell.

Most of the diesel railcars that came into operation were the Craven class, usually made up of two carriages and aimed at rural lines. Other models were also tried, including the one carriage Railbuses which were used for a time on the Braintree to Witham line. The first services to be used by diesel railcars were the lines out of Norwich Thorpe to Dereham, Wells and Lynn. They were soon followed by trains to Sheringham and Holt, to Yarmouth and local services to Ipswich. The following year, DMUs appeared on trains to Thetford and then from Ipswich to Saxmundham and Aldeburgh. Also, in 1957 they began to appear on branch lines to Harwich. I remember their introduction in 1958 on the Stour Valley line going through Sudbury as well as other lines radiating out from Cambridge and March.

By 1959 the transformation from steam to diesel was complete and revised timetables with regularised services could be fully implemented. The impact of these changes was seen within a few months with quicker journey times and fewer delays.

It is interesting to note that lines that only a few years later were to be axed under Beeching had considerable increases in revenue in the late 1950s and early 1960s. For example, on the line to Lynn there was an increase of 25%, and 50% between Wells and Norwich.

Although modernisation had been completed in East Anglia by the early 1960s, many diesel hauled trains were still hauling old fashioned carriages. Stations and signal boxes were still run in the same way. It was only the introduction of Paytrains that led to closure of most local booking offices on branch lines during this period.

Challenges for Drivers in Learning How to Drive Diesels

For many railwaymen, who had only known steam locomotives, learning how to drive diesel engines and diesel multiple units was a major challenge. The vast majority of drivers in the 1950s had no experience of being responsible for any other form of traction than steam. Few, for example, would have had experience of driving motor vehicles.

For the Eastern region, most drivers learnt about diesel electrics and multiple units at Ilford training school. Ken Welton, a driver based at Ipswich, wrote that many felt it was difficult to adjust to what was an alien form of propulsion which required different thinking. The first to be trained were the older drivers, often in their early 60s, who had no previous experience of how a diesel engine worked. Welton, with his fellow drivers had to learn to operate the Brush locomotive, the workhorse engine for the region from the 1960s onwards. After two weeks theory training at Ilford, they then had practical experience training on service trains. At first firemen were trained as drivers and spent months acting as assistants. They became much more experienced than drivers, given they were learning on the job over several months, compared with drivers who had about a month's training.[5]

Firemen grade was retained for a few years whilst steam was still in existence. They became known as secondmen, with new recruits starting as a driver's assistant, often acting as relief driver before becoming a permanent driver. The traditional 'starting role' of cleaner disappeared. These secondmen could draw on their previous knowledge as the heating system in the carriages still used a form of steam generator. Freestone remarks:

> A secondman could sometimes find himself constantly in and out of the engine room restarting a generator which had cut out, or resetting various trips etc. Sometimes he would even go as far as to wish himself back on a steam engine.[6]

Once electric heating was introduced, all main line passenger locomotives became single-operated. Single operation meant that relief drivers and crew were no longer responsible for coupling and uncoupling of the engines on arrival. Freestone makes the point:

> This was a big improvement for working conditions for a driver. He could now step off his train immediately upon arrival and know that he would not be required again until ten minutes before departure time.[7]

Twenty-five years later, drivers were again having to learn how to drive different locomotives, this time powered by electric. Electric trains were first used on the direct London to Norwich route in 1987, although they had been in operation to Colchester and Ipswich earlier than this. Freestone, now a permanent driver, tells us that basic training lasted for three weeks. One of the things the drivers had to learn and understand was how the power for these locomotives came from the overhead wires outside the engine. They had to know when there were gaps in the power coming from these wires. This meant knowing when to turn the engine off and on again. As Freestone noted, 'driving electric trains requires just that little extra concentration'. This is the reason why driving an electric train became an additional mental pressure rather than the physical side from the steam trains.[8]

For drivers like Ken Freestone, who was based at Ipswich, driving these electrics as well as diesels, was a very different experience to that of steam:

> For all their previous driving careers with steam they had complete control over their engines. They alone decided how much or little steam was required to cope with various routes over which they travelled. Now however they had merely to open a power controller after which automatic devices would come into operation in order to cope with the variable power demands. So, although a driver would still have to retain his old skills as regards road knowledge and the working of different types of trains, he was no longer the master of his own machine, as he had been in the past.[9]

This chapter has reviewed the changes from steam to diesel and electric and the impact it had on the workforce and the need for the development of new skills for the drivers. From the evidence of passenger numbers in the late 1950s and early 1960s there was the significant increase in use on many local lines. The DMUs particularly were very economical to run but this, in the end, did not save many lines from closure and it is to review the story of one such line that this volume now turns.

Notes

1 *A summary of the changes for the introduction of Diesel electric locomotives for the railway workforce in the Eastern Region can be seen in an article in BRER VOL.1. 1958 by K.Cook Main Line Diesel-Electric Locomotives.*

2 *Allen (1959) p.65.*

3 *BRER Jan 1960.*

4 *Allen (1959) p.49.*

5 *BTPF p.87-88.*

6 *Freestone and Smith (1998) p.198.*

7 *Ibid. p.201.*

8 *Ibid. p.206.*

9 *Ibid. pp.195-6.*

Saving The Stour Valley Line

If one was to compare a map of the railway network in East Anglia in 1948 with 1968, one would see a huge difference (see pages 146-147 for an example). By the late 1960s, whole swathes of Norfolk and Suffolk would no longer be served by any station at all. Major junctions, such as Melton Constable, no longer had any lines. Even popular seaside resorts, such as Hunstanton, Mundesley, Southwold, Aldeburgh and Brightlingsea, no longer had stations. There were no longer lines connecting major towns such as Cambridge, with Colchester; Kings Lynn with Norwich, or Bury St. Edmunds with Norfolk towns such as Thetford. Whilst many of these closures pre-date the 1960s, it was the proposed cuts introduced by Dr. Beeching, chairman of the British Railway Board in the 1960s, that are the most well-known.

This chapter reviews how one part of a line, the Stour Valley that linked Cambridge with Colchester, was closed and another saved as a result of a local campaign, and the arguments presented on either side by railway, commuters and local authorities. It is a story with strong personal associations. I was born and brought up in Sudbury, which was a main stopping point on this line and my father, Ernest Bourn, was a fireman and later driver on the route from the 1940s to his retirement in the late 1970s. He played a leading role in the campaign to retain the line. Today, the line from Sudbury to Marks Tey, which then links up with the mainline to Colchester and London, is a thriving and successful route. Due to the hard work of people, like my father with other railwaymen and commuters campaigning, we have a successful line today, and that Sudbury remains a thriving town, with less than 90 minutes by train from central London.

The Development of the Stour Valley Line

Plans for a line between Colchester, Sudbury, Bury St. Edmunds and Cambridge began in the 1840s but only the line from Marks Tey to Sudbury, linking to the line between Colchester and London opened in 1849. Ongoing battles between the various companies delayed further expansion until 1865, when the line was extended from Sudbury via Haverhill to Shelford, which then provided a link to the mainline from Cambridge to London. In the same year, a branch was extended from Long Melford, north of Sudbury, to Bury St. Edmunds. Another line, along the Colne valley linked Haverhill with Chappel and Wakes Colne, had already opened in 1863. Chappel was the next stop on the line from Marks Tey towards Sudbury and with the Colne Valley line this brought the market town of Halstead into the railway system.

In its early years, the Stour Valley line ran three to four trains a day each way. This was increased, in the 1890s, to six during the week. Freight traffic on the line reached its height at the turn of the century. This mainly consisted of agricultural produce from the rich arable hinterland, but coal, iron and gas from the North was also carried as well as barley and hops to supply a thriving brewing industry. Brickmaking, using the rich clay found in the region was also flourishing, bricks being transported by rail to other areas of the United Kingdom. Indeed, well known Victorian architectural wonders, such as the Royal Albert Hall, were built using bricks from Sudbury's kilns.

During the first decades of the 20th century, this branch line became an important railway link from the Midlands, via Leicester, Peterborough and Cambridge to the east coast. As many working families started to enjoy a week or fortnight's holiday, resorts such as Clacton, Walton, and via Colchester were accessible not just to Londoners. Travel to the continent, via Manningtree and Harwich from the Midlands using this line, became very popular between the wars.

As east coast holiday resorts boomed so did the line, and the 1930s saw the introduction of a summer Sunday service from Cambridge through to Clacton. This service continued to be popular in the years after World War II.

My father and mother moved from Melton Constable to Sudbury during the Second World War. During the war the line provided a vital transport link to the plethora of wartime airfields that were built throughout Suffolk, and later for transporting armaments for the war effort. There were more than a dozen airfields within a few miles of the branch line.

Sudbury Station in the 1940s and 1950s

Sudbury's connection to the railway not only offered logistical support to the armed forces, but was also a crucial way-station for the home front. Its station, with a large goods yard, held coal, crops and cattle on their way to the cities as well as barley and malt for nearby factories. Around the station were a gasworks, a brewer, electricity supply station and old chalk pits.

In the late 1940s, around 50 men were employed at Sudbury station—drivers, firemen, cleaners, porters and clerks. In pre-war days this had been as many as 75. It was an important hub with trains going from Sudbury to Colchester and to Cambridge in the other direction, and northwards to Bury St Edmunds via the branch at Long Melford.

Many lines benefited from the post-war nationalisation and the explosion of leisure travel. Throughout the summers of 1954 to 1966 there was a regular

Saturday express from Leicester carrying holidaymakers to Clacton on the Stour Valley line.

A goods locomotive going to pick up a wagon from a siding at Sudbury, 1955.

Despite this, in the 1950s, daily services were sparse. In the winter of 1955-6 there were only five through trains between Marks Tey and Cambridge and only three trains travelling from Long Melford to Bury St. Edmunds. The introduction of diesel railcars did lead to some changes. A number of shorter routes, including Marks Tey to Sudbury and Haverhill were introduced. Some services worked through to Ipswich, as well as Colchester, and travel times were cut.

Goods coming into Sudbury in 1950s.

This period reflected what was happening on many branch lines around the country. Sudbury station began to decline. By the end of the decade, the number of staff had been reduced to 15-20 commensurate with the decline in freight traffic. From being a thriving depot with staff employed in the booking office, goods depot, porters, signalmen, shunters, drivers and firemen, it could only maintain a skeleton staff by 1960. The majority of the personnel had worked on the line for most of their railway career. For example, Lewis George Austin (shown in the picture with the clock), had begun his railway career as a cleaner in North London in 1910 and moved to Sudbury ten years later where, after twenty years, he

Retirement presentation in 1957 for Lewis Austin, driver. He had served as a driver at Sudbury for over 30 years. My father is on the left.

became foreman-driver until he retired.[1]

The line during this period, from my own experience, had a lot of characters. The most famous was the Polish Princess, who was responsible for opening and closing the crossing gates at Rodbridge just north of Sudbury. Princess Madelin von Dembinska had taken the job while she tried to secure access to past family fortunes. She became the subject of a short Anglia Television film in 1961.[2]

The late 1950s also witnessed the biggest changes to date on the line with the end of steam and the introduction of diesel multiple units. The introduction of such trains was welcomed by drivers, like my father, because it meant you no longer left work covered in coal and soot and coughing from inhaling too much smoke. My father no longer needed to have baths every night.

The Sudbury station however required fewer staff. You no longer needed men to arrive at 5.00am to set the boiler alight for the first train ready to depart two hours later.

Changes in working patterns also affected other staff as well. Porters gradually disappeared and the introduction of diesel multiple units meant there was no need for turntables. Conductors could now walk easily through the train from one end to the other. This meant tickets could be bought on the trains negating the need for ticket offices at the local intermediate stations.

With the rise in road traffic, lines became increasingly vulnerable and the

Sudbury station workforce, 1949. My father is seated at the front second from the right.

first passenger service to go was between Long Melford and Bury St. Edmunds in 1961. The following year, its parallel line to the Stour Valley, the Colne Valley closed. Both of these closures led to reduced passengers on the Stour Valley itself, making it much more at risk.

Beeching Proposals

Dr. Richard Beeching was appointed as head of the British Railways Board in 1961 with the remit to return the railways to profitability without delay. The 1950s and early 1960s had been noticeable for a lack of public investment. Throughout the 1950s unprofitable lines had been closed, but with Britain's first motorway, the M6 Preston bypass being opened in 1958, followed in November 1959 by the first section of the M1, the motorway age had dawned. Railways were in a vulnerable position and rural branch lines were the most obvious place to make cuts.

What changed with the appointment of Beeching and the creation of a new Railway Board was a belief that all lines had to be based on efficiency, economy and safety of operation. The Board made often unfounded assumptions about branch lines, suggesting high overhead costs without any intention of looking for ways to reduce them.

Structures were created to deal with proposals for closures with Area Transport Users Consultative Committees established to deal with objections and submit reports to the Minister of Transport.

While it was assumed by many in the railway industry that the appointment of Beeching and the creation of these new structures would lead to closures and reductions in services, the proposals, when, in 1963, they were announced in the *Reshaping of British Railways*, was a complete shock. The report recommended the closure of a third of the rail network, with many cross country and rural services being axed. 2363 stations were proposed to be closed.

The Conservative government of the time supported the plans despite widespread public outcry, arguing that buses could provide a cheaper and more effective service. In 1964, with the return of a Labour government, it was hoped that the cuts could be reversed but instead closures began in earnest.

Closure of the Sudbury to Shelford Lines

The Beeching report recommended the closure of the entire line from Cambridge to Marks Tey. This came as a great shock to local councils, business groups and regular passengers on the line. Whilst there had been decline in support for the line during the 1950s and early 1960s, there was outrage from many groups because towns on the line, such as Sudbury and Haverhill, were undergoing major expansions in population and industry as 'new towns' created to solve the housing crisis in London.

It had not been realised that under-investment in British Railways since nationalisation had systematically run down support for many rural lines. Priorities now lay elsewhere and the rapid expansion of car owning families meant that unprofitable lines, with no more than three or four trains a day, were no longer feasible.

More and more freight was also being transported around the country in lorries. For example, at Long Melford, without any discussion with the local railway staff, a lorry loading dock was built by the Maltings right next to the railway line. Although local railway staff complained about the inevitable effect on the need for freight, regional and national managers within British Railways were not prepared to take on the influential road lobby.

By the early 1960s, the goods depot at Sudbury had closed with the final closure of goods traffic along the line in 1966. This was despite an indication by British Railways, in 1963, that freight services were secure for at least twenty years. By this time only four trains a day were making the complete journey from Cambridge to Colchester, two from Sudbury to Cambridge, and six between Marks Tey or Colchester and Sudbury. For people using the line from the rural villages, getting to and from major towns for the day became increasingly difficult by train.

Rural lines, such as the Stour Valley, employed a lot of staff, including people manning the level crossings and the various signal boxes. During the 1950s and 1960s, automatic gates and signalling were gradually being introduced elsewhere but there was no attempt to even consider such improvements on the line.

Fight to retain the line

Opposition to the proposed axing of the line grew quickly with local businesses and local councils leading the campaign. Action Committees were formed along the line.

During 1964, plans were drawn up by British Railways to start implementing the closure of the line, which would lead to 66 employees being made redundant. A leading campaigner against the closure of the line was Mick Cornish, councillor in the Sudbury area and prospective Labour candidate for Saffron Walden. He kept saying the Labour Party, when it got into power, would retain the line. But despite Labour winning the General Election that year, there was no radical change of policy. There were, at first, reassuring noises from the Minister of Transport at the time, Tom Fraser, but in 1965 plans for closure continued.

The stages necessary for closing lines during this period meant that there was a consultation process that involved the Transport Users Consultative

Council and their committees (TUCC) with meetings open to the public to hear objections. In April 1965, notices went up in all stations along the line that it would close subject to consultation and submission of objections by June of that year.

What had become evident throughout 1965 was that British Railways was beginning to reconsider the closure of the Sudbury to Marks Tey line. Passenger numbers were increasing with a growing number of London commuters moving to the area.

The campaign against closure was gaining momentum by May 1965 with over 750 objections being formally lodged with the Transport Users Consultative Committee. This meant plans to close the line later that year were immediately frozen.

The inquiry opened in Sudbury in August and clearly the proceedings resulted in some very volatile behaviour, with the police being called on more than one occasion. Objections came from well-known local businesses, commuters and occasional travellers on the line.

A leading figure in the campaign at this time was the Reverend Brian Bird, who worked closely with my father. Evidence that the line had been allowed to be run down, presented in remarks made at the inquiry by Revd. Bird, clearly came from my father.

In November, the report from the TUCC was published. It recognised the increased use of the Sudbury to Marks Tey section and that its closure would result in severe hardship. As a result, this section of the line was to remain open. It is clear that the Sudbury objectors had done well to galvanise many organisations, business and community groups against the closure. The local council, and in particular Sudbury's Mayor, local businessman, Geoff Kisby, had run a very professional campaign.

But, to the dismay of many campaigners and community groups, the rest of the line to Cambridge, including the rapidly expanding town of Haverhill, was to have no rail link. The Consultative Committee argued here that any hardship could be offset by existing and proposed additional bus services. Although there was anger at the closure of the line from local councils, a telling comment from a member of the Haverhill Chamber of the Commerce at this time said that the closure, whilst a disappointment, was not a surprise.

Despite the result of the inquiry, there was still hope, in 1966, that the Cambridge to Sudbury section might not close. Although the TUCC had recommended closure, the final decision rested with the Ministry of Transport who decided to ask for comments from the recently created East Anglian

Planning Committee. The signs were not good, as in August 1966 all purchasing of tickets at Sudbury and Haverhill was withdrawn.

Barbara Castle who was Minister of Transport in 1966 finally made her decision in September of that year regarding the recommendations of the TUCC. As anticipated, the line from Sudbury to Shelford, which then joined the line to Cambridge was to close but the line from Sudbury to Marks Tey would remain open.

At the end of 1966 a delegation of representatives from the local authorities around the Haverhill area met the General Manager of Eastern Region, Gerard Fiennes. It had become clear that he was interested in considering other options, including these local authorities subsidising the line.

There had been considerable debate about the rationale for closing the Sudbury to Shelford line. Haverhill was a rapidly expanding town during this period, with an influx of families from the London area. The evidence showing that the line was losing money was continually being challenged by a well-organised campaign committee. For example, during the discussions, British Railways suddenly revealed, in January 1967, that the line's anticipated loss was double that previously quoted, up from £26,000 to £52,000. The reason given was the poor condition of the track. The local authorities did agree to support the running costs at the lower figure. But this revised figure was too much for the them. What became apparent was that British Railways were determined to close the line.

The route from Shelford to Sudbury was closed on 4 March 1967. The last train was unfortunately taken over by Sudbury Round Table, in a rather odd fashion which turned the event into a 'wake' with coffin and fancy dress. As one regular passenger commented on this affair:

> I was flatly disgusted. If the people who travelled on the train had expended only a quarter of their energy in an attempt to save the line... we would still have a rail link to Cambridge.[3]

Twenty-one people lost their jobs, mainly level-crossing keepers but also signalmen. My father was one of the lucky ones. His job was retained, although the number of staff located in Sudbury was reduced to single figures and soon became just him and another driver, Sid Wacey. They alternated between early and late duties.

The closure of this line meant that places that were beginning to attract tourists, such as Long Melford, Cavendish and Clare, no longer had rail links. Haverhill, which today has a population of over 25,000, has no rail link with its nearest station being more than 25 miles away.

Reprieve but by no means safe

Although the Sudbury to Marks Tey line had been reprieved, there was no indication that British Railways were going to do more than to keep it open at minimum cost. A statement from the Ministry of Transport in 1966 said that, although the line was being retained, it would be subject to further review. There was still a need for continued vigilance and, as will be shown, there were further attempts to close the line in the succeeding years.

The need to keep a close eye on developments was demonstrated by the removal of all station staff on the branch line apart from Sudbury. In place of station masters there was now only one station manager and his deputy for the entire line.

By 1966, tickets for passengers could only be bought on the train. The change in role from guard to conductor-guard was not well received by all and many former guards found collecting money and the issuing of tickets a real challenge.

There was no systematic review of where potential savings could be made that would not affect passenger support. My father noted, in correspondence with the Chair of the campaign group in 1967, that savings could have been made by making redundant signal boxes and level crossings automatic. He also believed that the rail management were showing little or no interest in looking at any alternative but to close the line. The needs of passengers were being ignored with no amenities on any of the stations and no attempt being made to organise a timetable that would enable a connection north of Colchester.

British Railways had little interest in promoting the line or encouraging passenger numbers increase. The timetable was not displayed at most stations and stations were simply left to decay. Sudbury became an unmanned halt with no staff to service the platforms or buildings.

Campaign to Keep Sudbury to Marks Tey Line Open

There were several attempts by the British Railways Board in the years following the decision to retain the line to close it. In 1968, they published proposals for the closure. There was vociferous opposition and a ill-tempered meeting of the Transport Users Consultative Committee in July 1969.

Further attempts to close the line were made in the early 1970s. In 1972 closure plans were drawn up again, but the fuel crisis during this period resulted in a re-think of the road versus rail debate and the line was saved. It all pointed to a strategy by the management of British Rail, responsible for the line and the region, to let the Stour Valley line fail. There was no attempt by British Rail to develop a vision for the line which was surprising given that both Sudbury and Haverhill had already, from the early 1960s, been designated as towns for major expansion with relocating families from London.

What the campaign to save the line shows is that a strong and professionally run campaign, with support from leading businesses and local political figures, can result in success.

Success and Retention of the Line

Although the Sudbury to Marks Tey line was retained, it continued to suffer from under-investment. The rolling stock of diesel multiple units remained the same. By the 1990s it was being nicknamed the 'misery line' because of frequent delays and breakdowns. The track had remained the same since the 1930s.

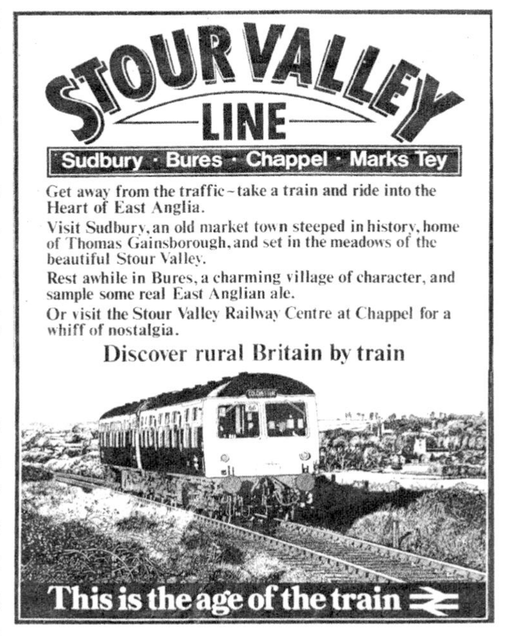

Stour Valley Line promotional poster.

A clear example of this lack of investment was the state of Sudbury station. *Rail News*, in 1976, noted that its windows were shattered and subject to periodic bouts of vandalism.[4]

Attempts were made during this period by commuters to promote the line. Mike Davies, a regular commuter during this period, set up a commuters' group that did a great deal to promote the line, organising special trains and making sure British Rail promoted the line. The group made a big difference with its focus on promoting the value of the line, rather than just acting as a lobby group to British Rail.

They organised surveys in 1975 and 1976 to show how important Sudbury and South Suffolk was in attracting commuters wanting to live in a rural location while working in London or Colchester. During this period, their research showed between 200 and 300 regular commuters using the line on weekdays. The group organised publicity campaigns to encourage people to use the line for shopping trips to Colchester, as a way of building up a Saturday service. They succeeded in getting the service extended to St. Botolphs (now named

Colchester Town) which was a lot closer to the main shopping centre than the mainline Colchester North station. They also succeeded in introducing a series of successful 'Santa' specials in the lead up to Christmas. The group organised 'seaside specials' to the Norfolk resorts in the 1980s. One of the reasons for the success of this group was they developed a positive working relationship with the area railway management, offering constructive suggestions that could improve the service.

Sudbury station had a short-lived role as a rail museum but with numerous arson attacks on and around the station it was eventually demolished and a new terminus was built. This new station, little more than an end-of-line halt, opened in October 1990. Built adjacent to the site of the former station, in hindsight, it could have been nearer to the centre of the town. Just two hundred yards closer, the station would have been more visible to shoppers in the town and closer to the bus station. Despite these reservations, the mere creation of this new station saw the start of a major turning point in the fortunes of the line.

By 2000, the line was gaining wider support and increasing its passenger numbers. There was also the introduction of new class 150 trains, automated information systems and an all year-round Sunday service. By 2002, 276,000 passengers were using the line. In 2006, the line became designated as a 'community railway' and became part of the Essex and Suffolk Community Rail Partnership network. This Partnership, which is designed to promote rural branch lines in the region, plays an important community role and benefited from the support and funding of local councils.

The Gainsborough line

Today the line, now renamed the Gainsborough, after the famous painter who was born in Sudbury, is one of the best performing in the country. Sudbury station has more passengers than Bury St. Edmunds, a much bigger town in West Suffolk. At a recent Suffolk Rail Policy Group meeting it was revealed that journeys have increased by 76% since privatisation with full-fare paying customers increasing by 148%, reduced-fare customers by 75% and season ticket holders up by 62%.

The line goes through some of England's most beautiful countryside, following the river Stour to Bures and then climbing to Chappel and Wakes Colne, over a very impressive viaduct, before it descends to Marks Tey where it joins the mainline from Colchester to London.

Along the way Chappel and Wakes Colne has become a popular stopping point, as it today houses the East Anglian Railway Museum, which has an excellent exhibition of the history of the line and offers the chance to view some

Sudbury station with new rolling stock today.

impressive old steam engines. The station is also home to the former foot bridge from Sudbury station, which joins the branch line platform with the museum platforms. (Further details about this museum can be found in the chapter on Heritage Lines.)

Today there is an hourly service in both directions from Sudbury to Marks Tey and a seven day-a -week service, meaning eighteen trains per day from Marks Tey to Sudbury during the week and 15 per day on Sundays. This compares with 4 per weekday in 1869, 10 in 1915, 6 in 1945 and 10 in 1985.

Like many lines, it has continued to have its incidents. On 27 January 2006, at least four passengers were slightly injured when a Class 156 train ran into the buffers at the Sudbury terminus. The cause of this incident appears to have been driver error. Rural lines have many crossings that require the drivers of vehicles to ring ahead before crossing the line. On 17 August 2010, at Little Cornard, a lorry driver failed to do this and collided with an oncoming train. The train driver and four passengers were seriously injured in the accident.

But these incidents have not detracted from what is a thriving line. The track was upgraded in the 1990s to modern long-weld flat bottom rails. At present the maximum speed on the line is 50 mph but upgrading it to enable faster speeds is unlikely since it would present a number of challenges particularly as the trains would have to go at much lower speeds through crossings at Cornard and Bures. However, January 2020 saw the introduction of the new bi-mode trains which can be powered by diesel or electricity. They are three coach trains and have more seats, wifi and better information screens.[5] This has resulted in a much more comfortable and smoother ride for passengers.

Notes

1 *Presentation to Sudbury Railwayman, Suffolk Chronicle and Mercury, April 26 1957.*

2 *http://www.eafa.org.uk/catalogue/98971; http://hysterical.foxearth.org.uk/2019/08/the-princess-level-crossing-keeper.html*

3 *East Anglian Daily Times (1967) Funeral of last Stour Valley Train Became Quite a Jolly Affair, March 6 1967.*

4 *Ward (1976) Eastern Halt Faces a Bitter Struggle for Survival, Rail News,March 1976,p.16*

5 *https://www.greateranglia.co.uk/about-us/news-desk/news-articles/new-trains-start-passenger-service-sudbury-marks-tey-route; https://www.eadt.co.uk/news/sudbury-line-gets-new-trains-1-6476329*

Changing Cultures: From British Rail to Privatisation

All the evidence suggests that many railway workers had a great sense of pride in their job. There was also a sense of identity with their particular region. This was especially strong prior to nationalisation in 1948 when there were still four main independent companies in operation. Even though nationalisation united the service into one, there was still a sense of regional identity among the workforce.

Nationalisation—Under Investment and Decline

Post-nationalisation aspects of the pre-war culture remained long past 1948, but there was clearly a more professional management system and workers could now more easily transfer to other posts further afield. However, for many railway workers in East Anglia nationalisation was a period of under-investment at a time when modernisation was desperately needed. While in the 1950s, technology moving from steam to diesel and electric, many of the working practices were still old-fashioned. In rural East Anglia it was exemplified by level-crossing keepers, a station master, porters, and clerks at every station, and a manned signal box at every place where tracks overlapped. The Beeching cuts were relatively easy to make rather than modernise these out-dated systems.

Despite the Beeching cuts, which had slimmed down the railway system, the continued lack of investment meant improvements in the quality of the services were minimal compared with elsewhere in Europe, such as France or Germany.

There are some interesting insights into the lives of railway workers during this period. Gerard Fiennes' role as a senior manager for the Eastern Region is quite revealing. He was a proponent for wanting an efficiently run railway system and was prepared to consider subsidising lines if the local authorities provided the funding. He believed that a viable railway system could be achieved with the use of diesel multiple

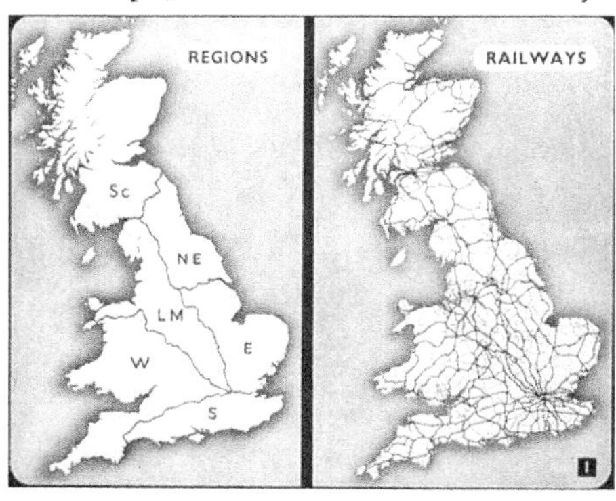

British Railways regions and main routes.

units that usually required minimal repairs. To his credit he played a major role in securing the retention of the East Suffolk line against the recommendation of Beeching. However, he increasingly came up against management bureaucracy and his candid account of his life on the railway led to his eventual resignation in the late 1960s.[1]

Prior to privatisation there were already moves to centralise management control with less emphasis on the needs of the workforce. Nationalisation made this inevitable and by the 1980s Roger Taylor, in his memoir, saw the introduction of Driver Only Operations (1988) as the 'death-knell of the railway as I knew it'.[2]

Change to a national structure came in the 1980s when the old regional divisions of British Railways were replaced by three passenger business sectors: Inter-City, London and South East (which became Network South East in 1986) and Provincial, later called Regional railways. Without doubt, this re-organisation resulted in increased efficiency and profitability. For example, Network South East, under the enterprising leadership of Chris Green, saw innovative developments such as travel cards, enabling people to make multiple journeys with one purchase, along with other customer driven improvements. Within no time at all the sector was breaking even.[3]

Privatisation

The 1990s saw another significant change—privatisation of the railway industry. This created separate for-profit companies, operating under a franchise, for each region and clear distinctions being made between those responsible for the running of the trains and those responsible for the maintenance of the track. In addition separate companies were created for freight traffic. The train companies could lose their franchise if they did not meet the expectations of passengers or government. In East Anglia this meant a succession of private companies running the passenger service. These included *National Express* and *First Group*, before ownership came under the control of *Abellio* in 2016, a Dutch based company.

Privatisation introduced competition and this filtered down to the workforce. Managers were recruited from other industries and several supervisors I spoke to mentioned that there were significant changes in working practices. Rather than working on the railways being a job for life, every post was competitive and there was much less job security than under British Railways days.

Whilst many railway workers still came to the industry with a passion and enthusiasm for trains, their working lives became determined by performance targets rather than any zeal governing success in the job. Such a system meant that individuals were , often moved from one post to another all too quickly.

This change of culture also changed the perception of being a train driver. Roger Taylor emphasises that the job was no longer seen as the "schoolboys' dream". He writes:

> The modern train driver has many roles and responsibilities, but their main purpose is to drive trains in a safe, punctual and economical manner in accordance with the Rules and Regulations. It is now a driver's responsibility to be aware of, and comply with, the Business Standards of their particular Railway Company to enable them to improve customer satisfaction.[4]

Taylor goes on to say that 'Woe betide any driver who falls sick or feels he does not meet the exacting standards required of him'. The driver has to recognise that they were regularly monitored for their attendance levels and he suggests that the environment was no longer as relaxed as it used to be. Today the driver is responsible for many activities, including making announcements on the train and tthere are very strict health and

The changing livery of trains in the Eastern region since privatisation.

Top: Train at Norwich showing the 'Anglia' branding, 2003.
Middle top: Train at Cambridge showing the "One' branding, 2004.
Middle bottom: Southend train at Liverpool Street showing the National Express livery, 2009.
Bottom: Lowestoft train at Ipswich showing the Greater Anglia livery, 2013.

safety regulations. Taylor concludes:

> Privatisation has a lot answer for, as it has broken up the railways into too many disaffected departments. A driver may work for a certain Train Operating Company, whereas the controlling signaller will be working for Network Rail… The main criteria these days are the performance figures, and the blame culture has resurfaced in some departments, because somebody has to pay for the delays and disruptions.[5]

Wolmar, in his review of privatisation on the railways, notes that contracting out work was changing the whole culture of the railway.[6] Many of those working on the railways were now casual workers who felt no allegiance to the industry. In many ways it was a return to the early years of the railways, with an itinerant workforce going around the country from one job to another.

East Anglia suffered more than many regions of England as a result of privatisation. Not only was there a succession of different companies running the trains in the region, the delay in introducing new rolling stock (until early 2020) and a succession of weekend closures, gave the service a bad reputation. Jokingly, it was even named Network Rail's least satisfied customer! However, the Managing Director of the railway in the region commented in early 2020 that 2019 had been a profitable year for the company.[7]

This chapter has shown the changing culture of the railway industry in the UK in the latter decades of the 20th century and the impact of privatisation which transformed ways of working. Long gone was any sense of collective or corporate identity. Working on the railways, particularly for drivers, had become a very individualised existence.

Notes

1 *Fiennes (1973).*

2 *Taylor (2008) p.107.*

3 *Wolmar (2007) p.296.*

4 *Ibid 2. p.119.*

5 *Ibid. p.120.*

6 *Wolmar (2012).*

7 *https://www.railmagazine.com/news/rail-features/exclusive-interview-we-are-feeling-positive-greater-anglia-md-jamie-burles*

Manningtree

This station, on the main line to London, is one I have got to know well since the late 1990s by being one of its regular commuters to London from Manningtree. Manningtree remains the junction to Harwich and, was until the 1970s, a major freight depot, with wagons coming and going from the nearby plastics factory. Today it is one of the busiest stations on the mainline with over 1 million passengers a year, an increase of over 50% in just over a decade.

Important Station on the Line from London to Norwich

Manningtree station, although technically in Lawford, opened in 1846 as part of the line linking Colchester to the south with Ipswich. The construction of the line was a major engineering challenge as it had to cross the River Stour estuary and a deep cutting was needed to the north of the station at Brantham. In 1854 the branch line was opened from Manningtree to Harwich giving access to the continent. Although the station appears, on first glance, to be a bit remote it is less than a mile from Manningtree town itself and not far from nearby tourist spots, such as Dedham and Flatford Mill, near the home of the artist John Constable.

Like many stations in the 19th century, Manningtree had a goods yard as well as being a passenger station. Many yards used horses to move wagons from one line to another. In February 1874 it was the scene of a tragic accident when a boy employed as an 'under horseman' was moving a horse box from the Harwich branch terminus to the main line. He was killed when he slipped in front of the box. A few years later, there was another tragedy when a train left the rails when the track was being repaired. One person died and another was injured.

Manningtree old stable block shortly before demolition to make way for an extended car park.

Near Manningtree were two sidings worked by men based at the station. Keeble's Siding was that rare occurrence, a private siding to a farm owned by the powerful and influential Keeble family. Nearby was the

Brantham siding for the plastics factory. One of its main roles was to deposit coal for the factory as well as transport goods to London.[1]

Manningtree became famous, in the first decade of the 20th century, for the Margaret Moult story. She was a convent girl at nearby East Bergholt, but after seven years as a nun, she could no longer cope with the harsh daily regime. In 1909 she escaped to Manningtree station with a view to getting a train to London. As she arrived at the station, staff and sisters from the convent turned up and tried to take her back. She protested and the noise alerted the station staff, who came to her assistance. The station master took pity on the girl and paid her train fare to London. Her story became headline news and she became a famous celebrity, going on a lecture tour and writing a book about her escape.[2]

The cover of Margaret Moult's autobiographical account. It became a best-seller when published in late 1909.

Manningtree station between the Wars

Between the two world wars the station had about 25 staff, including a lad who looked after the horses, shunter drivers, signalmen, porters, platelayers, goods clerks and booking clerks. There were also two refreshment rooms, one on the 'up' and one on the 'down' platforms. Reflecting the stratification of society at the time, there were three waiting rooms, first class, third class and one for ladies. There was also a W.H. Smith bookstall.

The complexity of the track around the station during this period meant there were several signal boxes, one at each end of the station, one for goods traffic to the nearby factories and one at each end of the loop line. In 1924, three of these boxes, the loop lines ones and the one to the sidings, were taken out of use.

Signal Box at Dedham

Just before Manningtree station, on the south side, was a signal box at Dedham which was still there until the 1960s. Its isolated location meant that working here could be a lonely existence with long days and nights alone for the signal man. With no real amenities he relied on water from a nearby spring.

Brodribb described the unusual way the box obtained its coal for heating purposes:

> At Dedham, coal could only be obtained from passing locomotives, which was strictly against the rule. The signalman on nights would have two cups of coffee ready ... The newspaper train took time to offload the papers at Manningtree and this meant that the following goods (train) would get held at Dedham signalbox. The crew of the goods would be treated to tea or coffee in exchange for shovelfuls of coal.[3]

Although this signal box is no longer there, this sense of informality reflected the camaraderie of railway workers being prepared to support their colleagues in

Malcolm Root's painting 'Constable Country' shows the Britannia class 70003, 'John Bunyan', passing Dedham signal box.

all sorts of ways even though they were not supposed to.

Manningtree Station in the post-war period

Like many others in East Anglia, Manningtree station was a very busy station during the Second World War. More and more airfields were being built nearby and its closeness to ports like Harwich made it important. In 1953 East Coast Floods caused major damage to the lines around the station and the station's role began to diminish and soon became almost forgotten. In the 1970s a film at the time shows it was still using oil lit signal lamps. Also, it showed that the station still had two drivers shunting freight to and from the factory. There were porters, booking clerks, goods clerk and foremen. Manningtree also had a gang of twelve men whose job was to check and maintain the track between Ipswich and Colchester and on to Harwich.[4] But this complement of staff did not survive the decade. By 1979 the station staff consisted of just three senior railmen working a shift pattern through twenty-four hours. In addition, there were two others who acted as porters and two more for the shunting work that was still needed. There was now only one signal box, but even this did not last long into the 1980s, falling into disuse by 1985. Electrification was installed at Manningtree in the 1980s and at the same time all of the sidings and shunting work closed.

1980s to Present Day

It is as a commuter station that Manningtree is most popular today, alongside its connection for the branch line trains to Harwich. In 1982 there were only three commuter trains to London before 9.00am. By 2007 this had risen to ten before 9.00am and increased to seventeen by 2019. As a consequence, parking became a major issue and two extensions have been necessary in the last twenty years. In 2020 the former outbuildings, including the stables for horses, were demolished to enable yet more car park space. The expansion of the car park in 2020 meant there is now space for over 800 cars.

The hub of the station today is the Station Buffet, which provides an excellent array of snacks, drinks and hot food. It gets a mention in a volume on *Unusual Railway Pubs* which says it retains the 'affections of many' commuters and occasional travellers.[5] Today it has more of a functional décor than in the past, but is still a warm place to be waiting for a train on a cold winter's morning.

Manningtree is a good example of a station that only still exists because of its commuters. The branch line to Harwich remains popular and profitable. With London now being accessible by train in just under an hour, its main purpose seems to be to enable passengers to get to their workplace in London as quickly and efficiently as possible. The station however still provides a good service in

Manningtree station, 2015.

the other direction to Ipswich and Norwich due to its proximity to important tourist attractions, such as Constable country, Manningtree station remains a very busy and thriving place. More recently it has installed a bike hire facility for the occasional traveller or tourist.

Notes

1 *Freestone and Smith (1998) p.49.*

2 *Moult (1912).*

3 *Brodribb (2009) p.44.*

4 *Cleveland (2007).*

5 *Barton (2013) p.95.*

Heritage Lines

My father was not a fan of heritage railways! He saw them as a way of undermining existing railways. There is some evidence to suggest that, in the 1970s, the creation of the East Anglian Railway Museum at Chappel on the Stour Valley line was a distraction from ensuring that all lines remained part of an integrated network.

Now fifty years later, it could be argued that heritage railways have in themselves helped to sustain some existing lines and, that some, in the future, could well be re-integrated back into the national system. What is evident is that the heritage railway industry is very popular and its very existence supports a broader interest in trains from generation to generation.

As East Anglia was devastated by the Beeching cuts, many communities became supportive of campaigns by enthusiasts to keep a visible presence of railways where there might be none. As a result, there are today several well-run heritage lines that are not only popular in themselves but, due to their location, act as a potential boost for local lines.

Many heritage lines and centres were formerly part of the national rail network in the region, including the Mid Suffolk Light Railway[1], Wells and Walsingham Light Railway[2], Whitwell and Reepham Railway[3], Bure Valley Railway[4] and the Nene Valley Railway[5]. There is also a privately-owned railway museum near Burnham on Crouch in Essex.[6]

This chapter will review some examples of these heritage lines and their potential role in the future.

Mid-Norfolk Railway

The Mid-Norfolk is a well-run and highly respected heritage line based at Dereham, running a service to Wymondham. This enabled a link to the nearby station on the Norwich to Thetford line. This railway has ambitions to extend north of Dereham to North Elmham and County School and on to Fakenham. The trust celebrated its twenty-fifth anniversary in 2020.

The line was originally part of the Lynn and Dereham Railway and was opened during the height of the 'railway mania' era in 1847. In the early decades of the 20th century the line was well used by both passengers and freight. Dereham station, for example, had over ninety staff. But, like many rural lines in East

Class 101 at Dereham on the Mid-Norfolk Railway, 2010.

Anglia, it suffered from chronic under-investment. However, despite increased use during the Second World War, it suffered the same decline as other stations as a consequence of the Beeching cuts of 1969.

However, the line remained open to freight and there were various attempts in the 1970s and 1980s to restore passenger services. Despite occasional excursions from Norwich to Dereham, it was only the continued use of freight that kept the line in existence. The last freight train worked the line in 1987.

Through the 1980s thanks to local railway enthusiasts, and after various false starts, the Mid-Norfolk Railway Society was formed to re-establish a line from Wymondham to Dereham. This was successful and in 1998 the trains began operating again on the line.

There were a number of factors that helped to support the re-establishment of this line. First of all, the energy and commitment of local enthusiasts. Secondly, much of the infrastructure to support a line had not been destroyed, including stations in situ. Thirdly, various local authorities, including Norfolk County Council, Breckland District Council and South Norfolk District Council, were all supportive of its re-opening. Dereham station today is an impressive building and there is a regular weekend, and occasional weekday, services on the line from March to October.

The Mid Norfolk line is also seen as part of a major and very ambitious long-term concept to link Wymondham to Sheringham via Dereham and Fakenham and the North Norfolk Heritage line from Holt. This plan, called the Norfolk Orbital Railway, has growing support and small steps to purchase strips of land on the route have begun.[7] One of the driving forces behind this initiative is the Melton Constable Trust that aims to link Fakenham to Holt and the North Norfolk line (see below). Funding, along with the memories of past railway workers, has helped to keep this idea alive.

The North Norfolk Line: The Poppy Line

Of all the heritage lines in existence in East Anglia, it is the North Norfolk or Poppy Line which is perhaps the most important to me. It runs from Holt to Sheringham, and for the most part, on the old line from Melton Constable to Sheringham. This line holds some of my fondest childhood memories. As a family we used to take the train from Melton and go to Sheringham or Cromer for the day during our summer holidays. The line covers just over ten miles, starting at a new station and junction just outside Holt, at Kelling Heath. It then passes through Weybourne, which has an excellent railway bookshop, and on to Sheringham. It makes its way through spectacular countryside, including Sheringham Park, heathland, and ends with a wonderful view of the sea as it enters Sheringham itself.[8] The line is called the Poppy Line because for many years along the line poppies could be seen growing in adjacent fields to the line.

J15 0-6-0 65462 at Sheringham, 2006.

It has been called one of the five great heritage lines in England and has been a past winner of the Independent Railway of the Year award.

The line was part of the M & GN and the influence of one of its most important figures, William Marriott, can be seen in a specially named museum to his memory at the Holt/High Kelling terminus.

In the 1960s, funds were secured to purchase Weybourne and later Sheringham station and to begin the process of purchasing locomotives and rolling stock. A service began in 1975 between these two stations. In 1980 land was purchased just outside Holt at High Kelling to build a new station. The old station at Holt no longer existed and the line was now under tarmac forming a bypass around Holt. Trains to Holt finally ran in 1989. From 2000, with considerable financial support from the Heritage Lottery Fund, new engine sheds and a museum have opened. The line is very popular, and trains run most days apart from mid-winter—a combination of diesel and steam hauled trains. It also runs 'railway experiences' when members of the public can learn how to drive a train or use the signalboxes. In 2018 it added a sixth locomotive to its collection of steam and diesel engines.[9]

One of the reasons for the continued success of this heritage line is that it directly connects to the mainline from Sheringham to Norwich. All that divides the two is a level crossing.

Colne Valley Railway

On the Suffolk-Essex border is the Colne Valley railway which, although much smaller than the two Norfolk lines, nevertheless has a charm of its own. It has only a mile of track near to the village of Castle Hedingham and was previously part of the Colne Valley line that ran from Chappel to Haverhill via Halstead, which was a loop line from the Stour Valley line.

The first part of the line from Chappel to Halstead was opened in 1860 with an extension through to Haverhill opening three years later. During its existence, for about a hundred years, the line provided an important service for local businesses, particularly various brick works close to the stations along the line. For local residents the line became an important link to the seaside places of Clacton and Walton. The line closed to passenger traffic in 1961 although freight services continued until 1964. Like other areas in East Anglia a preservation society was established. By the early 1970s the Colne Valley Preservation Society had purchased land and a locomotive. Although progress was slow, a station was erected at a new site. It has remained a small but popular heritage line, offering short train rides for families as well as a miniature railway and exhibition area. This all exists despite attempts, in 2015, for the land to be sold for housing development. The line was saved as a result of a public campaign bolstered by a major grant of nearly £2 million in 2016 from the Heritage Lottery Fund. A feature of this grant was the installation of a training centre for apprentices and an expansion of its educational facilities.[10]

The railway is only open from March to October every Sunday and on occasional days during the week in school holiday times. One of the attractions of the line is that it offers a range of experiences for all members of the family, including rides on small scale railways, an interactive learning museum, a signal box and a travelling post office.

East Anglian Railway Museum

The fourth and final review in this chapter is the one I have most knowledge about. The East Anglian Railway Museum on the Stour Valley line is based at Chappel station, which is still served by the regular services from Sudbury to Marks Tey.[11]

The Mail Train, Colne Valley Railway, 2011.

This museum had its origins in the late 1960s with the creation of the Stour Valley Preservation Society. The organisation aimed to preserve the then recently closed line from Long Melford to Bury St. Edmunds. This was unsuccessful and the enthusiasts saw an opportunity at Chappel, which had a number of derelict goods buildings, to create a railway heritage centre.

Gradually this site developed, but there remained a tension with staff operating the line from Sudbury to Marks Tey. They were concerned that the aim of the enthusiasts was to take over the entire line. However, during the 1980s the site's focus turned to presentation and preservation of artefacts and the East Anglian Railway Museum was born. At this time a footbridge was relocated from Sudbury station, an engine workshop was also established and a signal box moved from Mistley.

East Anglian Railway Museum.

In 1991, the Museum secured charitable status and, with further funding from the Heritage Lottery Fund, has become one of the premier railway museums in the country with excellent exhibitions and opportunities for short rides for children on the trains. It is open throughout the year.

A feature of the museum is its restored goods shed, which has a vast array of railway memorabilia and can act as a venue for events.

One of the other attractions of the railway museum is that its location provides an excellent base for walks around the area. Next to the museum, and over the adjacent railway line, is the very impressive Chappel viaduct.

It is still hoped, amongst those responsible for the museum, to be able to run heritage trains on the line, although at present these do not include steam locomotives.[12]

Notes

1 *https://www.mslr.org.uk*

2 *http://www.wwlr.co.uk*

3 *https://whitwellstation.com*

4 *https://www.bvrw.co.uk*

5 *https://www.nvr.org.uk*

6 *http://www.mangapps.co.uk/?LMCL=xxS4fV*

7 *https://www.edp24.co.uk/news/holt-land-buy-signals-vital-step-for-norfolk-orbital-railway-campaign-1-2335463; https://web.archive.org/web/20141205065200/http://www.norfolk-orbital-railway.co.uk/; https://www.fakenhamtimes.co.uk/news/norfolk-orbital-railway-north-mid-melton-constable-holt-1-6243706*

8 *https://www.nnrailway.co.uk/history/*

9 *https://www.northnorfolknews.co.uk/news/north-norfolk-heritage-railway-new-locomotive-1-5611237*

10 *https://www.halsteadgazette.co.uk/news/north_essex_news/14949556.colne-valley-railway-preservation-society-secure-almost-2-million-in-heritage-lottery-funding/*

11 *https://www.earm.co.uk*

12 *http://www.rail.co.uk/rail-news/2011/east-anglian-railway-museum-to-run-on-main-line/*

Conclusion

My motivation for writing this book grew from reading a wide range of books, articles and other publications on railways in East Anglia combined with re-reading my mother's diaries from the 1950s up to her final years.

What I found in my mother's diaries were lots of detail of day-to-day life and the challenges she had as the wife to a train driver whose working life was hard, poorly paid and not conducive to a healthy lifestyle. This, to me, contrasted with the many railway books which seem to focus on a nostalgic perspective dominated with pictures of steam locomotives. What I didn't see in many of these publications was the human side of working on the railways and the impact it had on the lives and families of the workers.

This volume has aimed to redress some of this imbalance by focusing primarily on the lives of railway workers putting them, wherever possible, in a broader social context. What I have also tried to do is bring in stories and experiences from my own family and of places and lines that I know well. It is, in part therefore, a personal memoir of experiences with the railway.

What I learnt from researching and writing it was the pride railway workers, particularly drivers and firemen, had in their work. In many ways their approach reflected what the historian Eric Hobsbawm called a form of 'labour aristocracy'. The railways have always been run on a very hierarchical basis. Up until the introduction of diesel and electric motor power, there was a lengthy form of apprenticeship and a 'pecking order' when it came to promotion. I can remember that my father was working on the railways for eighteen years before he became a driver.

What the railways did however provide until, I would suggest, privatisation was a sense not only of pride but collective identity and solidarity amongst the workforce. Workers looked after each other and I know from my own father's experience that when his depot, Sudbury, had a significant number of staff, there were regular works outings and events. Another example, which my grandparents at Melton Constable benefited from, was the Railway Institute, an excellent social club for workers and their families.

At a broader social and economic level, this volume has aimed to show the development and impact of the railways on communities, the ways in which lifestyles changed and the opportunities travel provided to broadening peoples' horizons. The growth of the railways mirrored wider social changes, such as the gradual move away from an autocratic and almost feudal way of working to one that was more modern, if still rather hierarchical. Only as a result of hard-fought battles did the railway workers achieve better terms and conditions of employment. What has also been a long struggle has been to ensure that working on the railways was safe. For much of the 19th century, the railways, and this was particularly the case in East Anglia, were run on rather amateurish lines lacking any strategic direction.

East Anglia remains today a thriving region for tourism. It has some of the most beautiful countryside in England and many of its coastal resorts continue to attract visitors. The railways historically provided opportunities for families from industrial communities to experience fresh, clean air and the delights of superb beaches in Norfolk, Suffolk and Essex. Important industries, such as fishing and brewing, would not have grown in the region without the railways.

Today all of the lines in Norfolk, Suffolk and Essex are popular and successful. They all have new rolling stock and trains are on the whole reliable, clean and efficient. Many of the local lines are now well marketed with their own 'identities', such as the Gainsborough for the Stour Valley and the Mayflower for Manningtree to Harwich. The region today also has some excellent heritage lines and railway museums. These are very popular and provide a good introduction to the history of many of the lines. But there remains the danger that such heritage lines and museums might be unwittingly promoting the past as some form of 'golden age' of the railways. This volume has aimed to put a different perspective to the concept of the past golden age of railways. Even at a time when there were many more lines in the region than there are today, such as between the wars, it was not a period of success, comfort or profitability for the railways. Many of the trains ran with inefficient locomotives, uncomfortable carriages with poor working conditions for the drivers, firemen, guards and signalmen.

Both my father and grandfather enjoyed working on the railways. However this was in part due to the camaraderies and interaction with fellow railway workers and the general public rather than their working conditions or wages. Whilst today working conditions are much better and certainly the wages have significantly improved, a significant shift has been the impact of the increase in mental pressure. Driving a train with four hundred passengers on board at over a hundred miles an hour can be a very stressful occupation. Privatisation has exacerbated this even more by breaking much of the former collective spirit that existed on many of the lines. When I travelled with my father in his cab on the diesel multiple units in the 1960s and 1970s, I can remember the good humour of everyone—the respect and warmth given by passengers to my father and the guard on the train. As he checked with the guard that all passengers were safely on board, you knew you were going to have an enjoyable experience through beautiful East Anglian countryside. 'Right Away'.

Maps

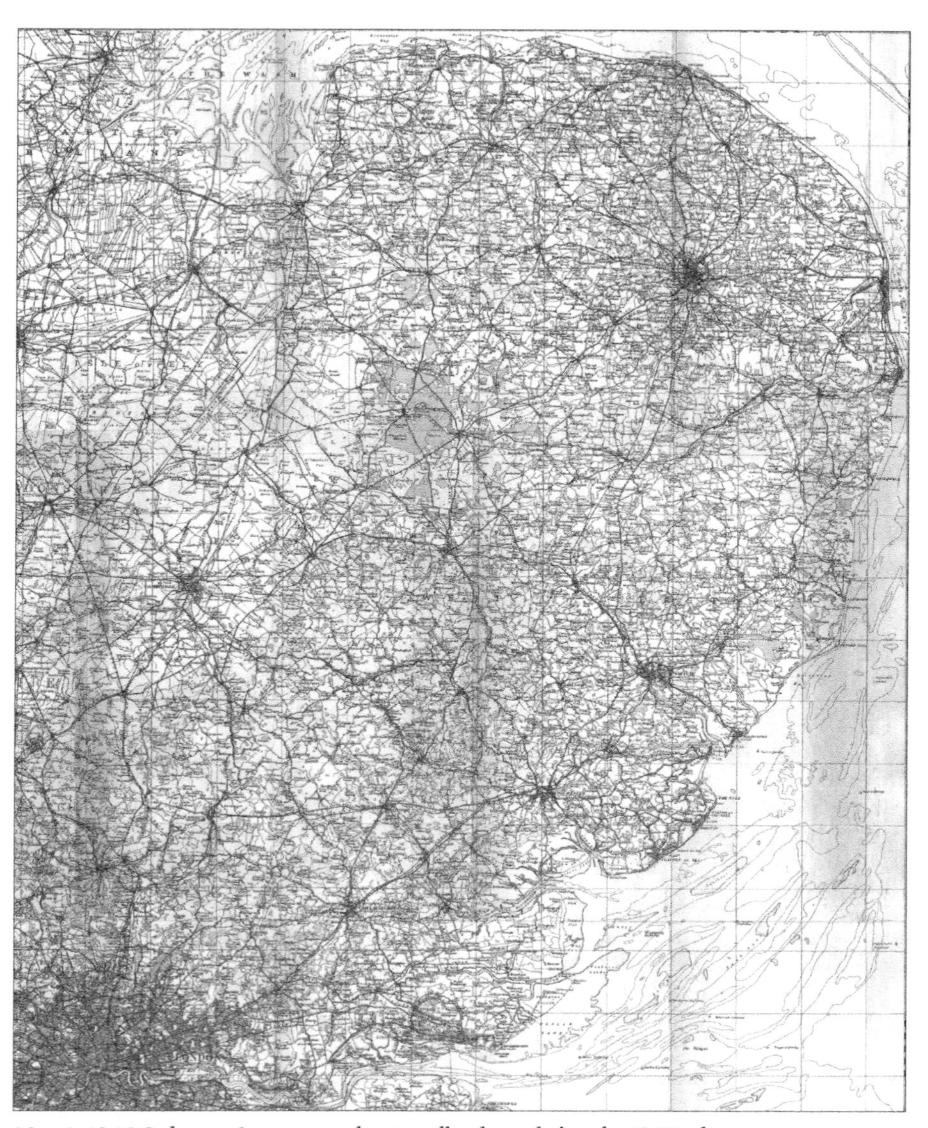

Map 4. 1946 Ordnance Survey map showing all railways before the 1960s closures.

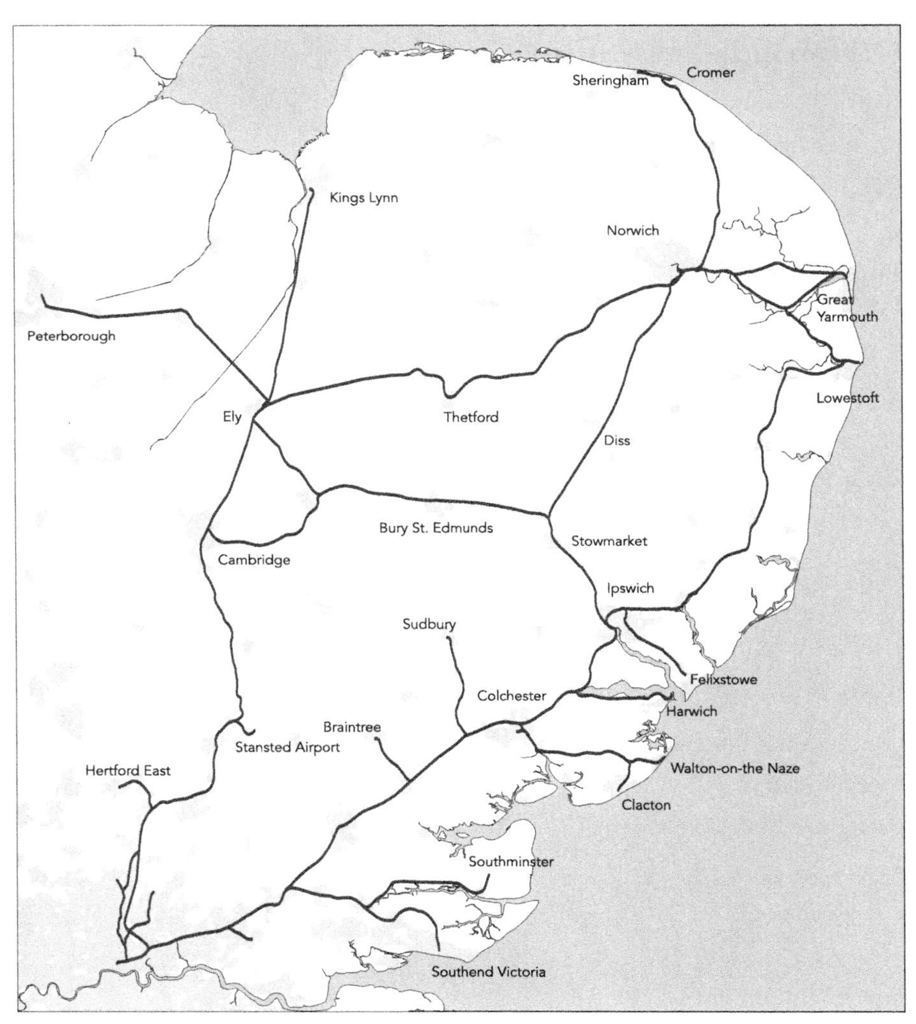

Map 5. Greater Anglia rail network, 2020.

Bibliography

Archives including Magazines

British Railways Eastern Region (BRER) Journal 1948-1963.

Great Eastern Railway (GER) Magazine 1911-1926.

LNER Magazine 1927-1947.

M & GN Circle Bulletin.

Railway Magazine 1949.

Railway and Travel Monthly 1910-1922.

M & GN Oral Histories.

Locomotive Magazine 1917.

National Archive of Railway Oral History (NAROH).

Steam World 2005.

Joint Line no.185.

Great Eastern Journal vols.17-19.

Suffolk Chronicle and Mercury.

Rail News 1976.

Websites:

www.broadlandmemories.co.uk

www.bvrw.co.uk

www.disused-stations.org.uk

www.eafa.org.uk

www.earm.co.uk

www.edp24.co.uk

www.fakenhamtimes.co.uk

www.gersociety.org.uk

www.greateranglia.co.uk

www.greatyarmouthmercury.co.uk

www.halsteadgazette.co.uk

www.harwichanddovercourt.co.uk

www.ipswichanddistricthistoricaltransportsociety.co.uk

www.lowestoftjournal.co.uk
www.mangapps.co.uk
www.mgncircle.org.uk
www.mslr.org.uk
www.norfolk-orbital-railway.co.uk
www.nnrailway.co.uk/history
www.norfolkrailwaysociety.org.uk
www.nvr.org.uk
www. preservedbritishsteamlocomotives.com
www.rail.co.uk/rail-news
www.railwaysarchive.co.uk
www.railwaywondersoftheword.com
www.wwlr.co.uk
www.youtube.com

Books and Articles

Adderson, R. and Kenworthy, G. (1998) *Branch Lines Around Cromer*, Midhurst, Middleton Press.

Adderson, R. and Kenworthy, G. (2007) *Melton Constable to Yarmouth*, Midhurst, Middleton Press.

Adderson, R. and Kenworthy, G. (2011) *South Lynn to Norwich City*, Midhurst, Middleton Press.

Alderton, D. (2005) The Chicken or the Egg? The Relationship Between Industry and Transport in East Anglia, *Industrial Archaeology Review*, 27:1,121-128.

Allen, C. (1955) *The Great Eastern Railway*, London, Ian Allan Publishing.

Allen, C.(1959) *Great Eastern*, London, Ian Allan Publishing.

Back, M. (2019) Clerical Staff Recollections, *Great Eastern Journal*, vo.18.10,38-41.

Baker, A. (2019) *A Life On the Rails*, Whitwell and Reepham Railway Preservation Society.

Barney, J. (2007) *The Norfolk Railway—Railway Mania in East Anglia 1834-1862*, Norwich, Mintaka Books.

Barton, B. (2013) *Unusual Railway Pubs, Refreshment Rooms and Ale Trains*, Wellington, Somerset, Halsgrove.

Beaumont, R. (2002) *The Railway King—A biography of George Hudson*, London, Headline Book Publishing.

British Transport Pensioners Federation (BTPF) (n.d.) *Memories—Behind the Scenes in British Transport—Collated by BTPF Anglia*, British Transport Pensioners Federation.

Brodribb, J. (1994) *The Eastern Before Beeching*, Shepperton, Surrey, Ian Allan Publishing.

Brodribb, J. (2000) *Branches and Byways East Anglia*, Shepperton, Oxford Publishing Co.

Brodribb, J. (2009) *The Main Lines of East Anglia*, Oxford, Ian Allan Publishing.

Brooks, E.C. (1997) *Sir Samuel Morton Peto Bt. 1809-1889, Victorian Entrepreneur of East Anglia*, Bury, Bury Clerical Society.

Brown, R.D. (1980) *East Anglia—1939*, Lavenham, Terence Dalton.

Burton, A. (2016) *The Railway Builders*, London, Pen and Sword Books;

Caton, P. (2013) *The Next Station Stop—Fifty Years By Train*, Kibworth Beauchamp, Matador.

Clark, R. (1967) *A Short History of the Midland and Great Northern Joint Railway*, Norwich, Goose and Son.

Cleveland, D. (2007) *Manningtree Station*, Manningtree, David Cleveland.

Coleman, T. (2000) *The Railway Navvies*, London, Pimlico.

Connor, J.E. (2003) *The Wreck of the Cromer Express*, Colchester, Connor & Butler.

Cox, J.G. (2008) *Samuel Morton Peto, 1809-1889—The Achievements and Failings of a Great Railway Developer*, Oxford, Railway and Canal Historical Society.

Dawes, D. (2019) Summer Saturday at Liverpool Street in 1951, *Great Eastern Journal* 179 July 2019.

Digby, N. (1993) *A Guide to the Midland and Great Northern Joint Railway*, Shepperton, Ian Allan Publishing.

Digby, N. (2014) *The Stations and Structures of the Midland and Great Northern Joint Railway, Vol.1*, Lydney, Lightmoor Press.

Digby, N. (2015) *The Stations and Structures of the Midland and Great Northern Joint Railway, Vol.2*, Lydney, Lightmoor Press.

Essery, R.J. (2009) *The Midland and Great Northern Joint Railway and its Locomotives*, Lydney, Lightmoor Press.

Fiennes, G. (1973) *I Tried To Run A Railway (2nd edition)*, London, Head of Zeus.

Freestone, J. and Smith, R.W. (1998) *Ipswich Engines and Ipswich Men*, Ipswich, Over Stoke History Group.

Gale, J. (2015) *The Coming of the Railways to East Anglia*, Ely, Melrose Books.

Garrod, T. (1997) *England's Most Easterly Railway—150 Years of the Lowestoft —Norwich line*, Lowestoft, Railway Development Society (East Anglian Branch), Lowestoft.

Gordon, D.I. (1964) *The East Anglian Railways Company: a study in railway and financial history*, PhD thesis, University of Nottingham.

Gordon, D.I. (1990) *A Regional History of the Railways of Great Britain Vol.5: The Eastern Counties*, Newton Abbot, David and Charles.

Hall, P. (2000) *Making an Exhibition of Myself: the Autobiography of Peter Hall*, London, Oberon Books.

Hardy, R.H.N, Bird, C., Butcher, D. (2011) *B12s Remembered*, Sheringham, Midland and Great Northern Society.

Harvey, D.W. (1986) Bill Harvey's 60 *Years in Steam*, Newton Abbot, David and Charles.

Hawkins, C. and Reeve, G. (1987) *Great Eastern Railway Engine Sheds, Part Two: Ipswich and Cambridge Districts*, Didcot, Wild Swan Publications.

Hewison, C.H. (1981) *From Shedmaster to Railway Inspectorate*, Newton Abbot, David and Charles.

Hilton, H.F. (1946) *The Eastern Union Railway, 1846-1862*, London and North Eastern Railway.

Howlett, P. (2004) The Internal Labour dynamics of the Great Eastern Company, 1870-1913, *Economic History Review, LVII*, 2 (2004), 396-422.

Jenkins, A.B. (1960) *Memories of the Southwold Railway*, Lowestoft, John. W. Holmes.

Joby, R.S. (1977) *Forgotten Railways Volume 7: East Anglia*, Newton Abbot, David and Charles.

Joby, R.S.(1987) *East Anglia—Regional Railway Handbooks*, Newton Abbot, David and Charles.

Lee, D., Taylor, A., Shorland-Hall, R., (2019) *The Southwold Railway, 1879-1929*, Barnsley, Pen & Sword.

MacDonald, P. (2017) *Rural Settlement Change in East Suffolk, 1850-1939*, PhD thesis, University of East Anglia.

Major, S. (2015) *Early Victorian Railway Excursions*, Barnsley, Pen and Sword Transport.

Major, S. (2018) *Women Railway Workers in World War 2*, Barnsley, Pen & Sword.

Marriott, W. (1974) *Forty Years of a Norfolk Railway*, Sheringham, M & GNSociety.

McCarthy, C. & D. (2007) *Railways of Britain—Norfolk and Suffolk*, Hersham,

Ian Allan Publishing.

McKenna, F. (1980) *The Railway Workers 1840-1970*, London, Faber and Faber.

Miller, T. & M. (2013) *Early Railway Happenings in South Norfolk*, Rollesby, Miller.

Mitchell, V. (2011) *Branch Lines to Harwich and Hadleigh*, Midhurst, Middleton Press.

Mitchell, V. (2012) *Branch Lines to Sudbury*, Midhurst, Middleton Press.

Mitchell, V. & Smith, K. (1984) Branch Line to Southwold, Midhurst, Middleton Press.

Moffat, H. (1987) *East Anglia's First Railways*, Lavenham, Terence Dalton Ltd.

Morris, R. (2012) *Iron in the Blood*, Cirencester, Memoirs Publishing.

Moult, M. (1912) *The Escaped Nun: the story of her life*, London, Cassell.

Neele, G.P. (1904) *Railway Reminiscences: notes and reminiscences of half a century's progress in railway working, and of a railway superintendent's life, principally on the London and North Western Railway*, London, McCorquodale & Co.

Oppitz, L. (1989) *East Anglia Railways Remembered*, Newbury, Countryside Books.

Paye, P. (2005) *The Snape Branch*, Usk, Oakwood Press.

Paye, P. (2008) *The Framlingham Branch*, Usk, Oakwood Press.

Paye, P. (2006) *The Hadleigh Branch*, Usk, Oakwood Press.

Paye, P. (2012) *The Aldeburgh Branch*, Usk, Oakwood Press.

Paye, P. (2018) *The Southwold Railway*, Lyndey, Lightmoor Press.

Pearson, C. (ed.) (2010) *E.J. Rudsdale's Journals of Wartime Colchester*, Stroud, The History Press.

Phillips, C. (1989) *The Tendring Hundred Railway—A History of the Colchester to Clacton and Walton Lines*, Colchester, Connor and Butler.

Rhodes, J. (1982) *The Midland and Great Northern Joint Railway*, London, Ian Allan Publishing.

Pendeleton, J. (1896) *Our Railways, Vol.1*, London, Cassell and Company.

Reynolds, M. (1881) *Engine Driving Life: Stirring Adventures and Incidents in the Lives of Locomotive Engine-Drivers*, London, Crosby, Lockwood and Co.

Robbins, M. (1967) *Points and Signals: A Railway Historian at Work*, London, Allen and Unwin.

Robertson, R. (1996) *Steaming Through The War Years*, Oxford, Oakwood Press.

Robinson, W.P. (2005) *From Steam to Stratford*, Horncastle, Cupit Print.

Ross, D. (2010) *George and Robert Stephenson*, Stroud, The History Press.

Strangleman, T. (2002) Constructing the Past: Railway history from below or a study in nostalgia? *The Journal of Transport History*, 23, 2,147-158

Suffolk Federation of Women's Institutes (1994) *Suffolk Within Living Memory*, Newbury, Countryside Books.

Taylor, R. (2008) *Train Driver—A Railway Career Memoir*, Bourne, Warners Group Publications.

Wallis, A.T. (2011) *Stour Valley Railway Through Time Vols. 1 and 2*, Stroud, Amberley Publishing.

Weaver, L.T. (1975) *The Harwich Story*, Harwich, Weaver.

Whitechurch, V.L. (1898) Cromer: The Goal of the Great Eastern Crack Expresses in *Railway Magazine June 1898*.

White, M.R. (2010) *Railways of Suffolk*, Lowestoft, Coastal Publications.

Wolmar, C. (2007) *Fire and Steam*, London, Atlantic Books.

Woods (2014) *Mid-Nineteenth Century Migration From Norfolk To London: Migratory patterns, migrants' social mobility and the impact of the railway*, Dissertation for an MA in Historical Research Institute of Historical Research.

Wragg, D. (2012) *Wartime On The Railways*, Stroud, History Press.

Wrottesley, A.J. (1970) *The Midland and Great Northern Joint Railway*, Newton Abbot, David and Charles.

Index

Printed in Great Britain
by Amazon